bistro latino

# bistro latino

Home Cooking Fired
Up with the Flavors of
Latin America

## Rafael Palomino
### with Julia Moskin

WILLIAM MORROW AND COMPANY, INC. *New York*

Library of Congress Cataloging-in-Publication Data
Palomino, Rafael, 1963–
    Bistro Latino / Rafael Palomino with Julia Moskin.— 1st ed.
        p.   cm.
    Includes index.
    ISBN 0-688-15503-0
    1. Cookery, Latin American.   I. Title.
    TX716.A1P35   1998                                          97-49353
    641.598—dc21                                                CIP

Printed in the United States of America

FIRST EDITION

1   2   3   4   5   6   7   8   9   10

BOOK DESIGN BY LAURA HAMMOND HOUGH

www.williammorrow.com

for martha

# Acknowledgments

Many thanks to:

- Rafael and Graciela Palomino, Gloria Moreno, Martha and Marina Arevalo, and Donna and Mario Gutierrez
- Jaime Suarez, Avi Najar, and Moe Gad at Bistro Latino
- Jane Dystel
- Pam Hoenig and Naomi Glikman at William Morrow
- Steven Hall and Sam Firer at Steven Hall Public Relations
- Larry Forgione, Jonathan Waxman, Bradley Ogden, Charlie Palmer, Douglas Rodriguez, and Gillian Duffy
- and especially Amanda Palomino, our traveling companion and tamale-maker

# Contents

# Introduction

What is Bistro Latino? Well, just to start . . . Bistro Latino is a plate of fresh, cool salmon tartare sparked with lemon and cilantro; it's a crisp, hot potato gratin infused with scallion, tomato, and milky farmer cheese; it's a deep, wine-dark oxtail stew brimming with potatoes and yuca. It's Ajiaco, flavor-rich Colombian chicken soup, briny with capers and smoothed with a dollop of sour cream; it's red snapper baked in a bright sauce of fresh tangerine juice, parsley, and mushrooms, served over steaming rice made fragrant and smoky with roasted corn and garlic. It's a classic flan scented with the tropical sweetness of passionfruit, and it's a mug of frozen chocolate mousse studded with crunchy bits of toasted cashew nuts.

As French home cooking is to French bistro cooking, so is South American home cooking to Bistro Latino: home cooking refined and reinvented, made vibrant and exciting but still simple, casual, and familiar. Full of the sun and the sea and the unmistakable flavors and aromas of the New World as well as the traditions of the Old, Bistro Latino is the way I believe many Americans—North and South—will be cooking in the twenty-first century.

I spent my childhood in Bogotá, the capital of Colombia, and moved with my family at age thirteen to New York City. When I was in high school in Queens, I never thought much about the food we ate at home and in the Colombian restaurants in the

Jackson Heights neighborhood that became my second home. Since my parents are both Colombian and both wonderful cooks, it was simply the only food I really knew; the techniques, tastes, and textures were part of me. It wasn't until long after I became a professional chef that I was able to figure out my own culinary orientation—to find my true "voice" as a chef—and when I did, no one was more surprised than my family that it was a combination of Mediterranean, French, American, and Latin influences!

In my years as a chef, I've noticed that Latin cuisine is easily and often dismissed by North Americans; some think it's all a version of Mexican food, others think it's just rice and beans, still others never think about it at all. The very idea of "Latin" cooking is a complicated one. Latin America stretches all the way from northern Mexico to the southern tip of Chile—a distance of over eight thousand miles. The Spanish-speaking islands of the Caribbean—Cuba, Puerto Rico, Santo Domingo—are also included in the "Latin America" designation. But while there are certain similarities in the language, culture, history, and cuisine of these regions, they're far outweighed by the many differences. Since my roots are in South America itself, that's where the "Latin" influences on my food come from—especially the cuisine of my native Colombia, though Peru, Brazil, and Argentina also make important contributions in my kitchen.

Of course, the story of Latin food traditions is tightly wound up with the dramatic and often tragic story of Latin America's civilizations, invasions, genocides, repopulations, immigrations, and revolutions. The bare framework of the story is this: In the year 1500, the vast forests, grasslands, and rivers of South America were barely disturbed by the continent's relatively small indigenous population. The empire of the Inca rulers was at its most extensive, encompassing Peru, Ecuador, Chile, Bolivia, and part of Argentina. In the rest of the continent, countless small hunting and fishing communities lived, generally separated by thick jungles and impassable mountains. A few larger "cities," such as Machu Picchu and Ciudad Perdida (northern Colombia's Lost City), served as religious, administrative, and cultural centers, but isolation and self-reliant communities were the norm.

The first Portuguese and Spanish *conquistadores* arrived (via the Caribbean and Mexico) at the end of the fifteenth century; Christopher Columbus's second expedition landed in northern Colombia in 1499. Those who followed Columbus quickly penetrated to the continent's Andean interior, spurred by reports of cities and mountains made of gold. They never found the El Dorado they sought (though the goldwork of the Tayrona and other native communities was truly spectacular); many died trying, and their quest for wealth grimly explains how the continent was conquered so quickly and brutally. Uncounted millions in gold were shipped from ports like Cartagena de Indios back to the crowns of Europe, and uncounted natives were murdered in battle, by disease, and through enslavement.

Prior to the European invasion, most of Latin America subsisted on some combination of corn, squash, potatoes, and beans. With chile and honey for flavor, plus smaller amounts of fish and shellfish, fruit, fowl (especially ducks), and rodents (especially rabbits and guinea pigs), they coaxed a cuisine from the difficult, often dry and mountainous land. But with the arrival of Europeans on the continent, everything quickly changed. Along with disease and destruction, the Spanish brought beef, lamb, goats, chickens, wheat, citrus fruits, sugarcane, nuts, and spices that, to varying extents, were adopted and adapted by the native population. Just as quickly, the foods of the New World began to make the return trip to Europe.

The influence of Latin ingredients on European cooking was immediate and tremendous. Without the contact between these two regions, there would be no potatoes, tomatoes, squash, corn, beans, chile peppers, chocolate, or vanilla in Europe. (Imagine it—no tomato sauces for pasta, no chocolate mousse, no potato *gratin,* no *cassoulet,* no polenta!) All these foods were well known to and highly developed by the indigenous populations of South America. Potato cultivation and cuisine, especially in Peru, were extraordinarily sophisticated; the populations of both Mexico and Peru used corn in hundreds of different ways. Without these starchy, filling staples, the cuisines of Europe and North America would be infinitely poorer in variety, flavor, and nutrients. Although the French, Italians, and Spanish were wary at first—both potatoes and tomatoes were used merely as decorative houseplants for decades after their arrival in Europe—enthusiasts like the French botanist Auguste Parmentier and gourmand Brillat-Savarin ensured their eventual acceptance by European palates. Soon after, European immigrants to the New World started to bring potatoes and tomatoes *back* to the Americas, in new dishes that became part of the wonderful diversity of American cooking.

Eighteenth- and nineteenth-century immigrants to South America—the French and Austrian colonizers who ruled under the infamous Emperor Maximilian and Empress Carlotta, the Arab traders who plied along the Atlantic coast, the Portuguese who subdued and settled Brazil, the African slaves imported to work the mines and plantations, and the Chinese workers on the Andean railroads—also engaged in this kind of culinary give-and-take. *Cocina criollo*, or Creole cuisine, is synonymous with "local cooking" all over Latin America, but it means different things in different lands. The term *criollo* was originally a racial category invented by the Spanish to refer to (and to discriminate against) whites of Spanish blood who were born in Latin America rather than in Spain. (Other categories were *mestizos*—those of European and Indian blood; mulattos—of

European and African blood; and zambos—of African and Indian blood.) But *criollo* has come to be a proud designation for anything that incorporates many sources of Latin America's people and culture. Today, every part of the continent has its own *cocina criollo*—with major Dutch influences in Venezuela, Portuguese in Brazil, and Japanese in Peru.

As I learned while studying the cooking of Latin America, an entire chapter could be written about many of the dishes in this book, especially those considered *criollo*. To take just one example, ceviche is a distinctively Latin dish of raw fish marinated until "cooked" in citrus juice. It's especially identified with the cuisines of Ecuador, Mexico, and Peru. Culinary historians agree that it is a very old native dish, but citrus didn't arrive in the New World until the Spanish and Portuguese conquistadors did; no one knows quite how ceviche was made safe and palatable before that. Onions, another European food, are absolutely integral to the dish today. Yet ceviche is most often served with corn and sweet potatoes, definitely native to the Americas. And finally, the technique of cooking with acid suggests a possible Asian origin.

Like that of other Latin countries, Colombia's cooking today is a rich brew of indigenous, Iberian, African, Asian, Caribbean, and North American influences. Although the cuisine of Colombia varies tremendously according to the terrain (seacoast, mountains, and fertile river valleys) and population, some dishes have become nearly universal. Colombia's dizzyingly varied *cocina criollo,* with its strong African and Spanish influences, informed my childhood in the cosmopolitan capital of Bogotá. Antioquía's *plato montañero,* a ribsticking combination of rice, red bean stew, pork rind, fried plantains, and avocado, has become popular all over the country and is truly Colombia's national dish. (Like Americans with hamburgers and fries, Colombians never seem to tire of *plato montañero*.) Banana leaf–wrapped tamales and golden empanadas are everywhere. These are the foods of my childhood, and when my family arrived in New York I was delighted to find them transplanted here to the States, just as I had been. The Latin restaurants of New York City are dedicated to making many immigrants feel at home, and it's not unusual to see ten or more different "ethnicities" of tamales or empanadas (Chilean, Colombian, Dominican, and more) in the window.

My extended Colombian family is based in Bogotá—and, like most Colombians, they take cooking very seriously. Discussions of classic Bogotano specialties like *Ajiaco* (page 106), *Changua* (page 98), and *Sobrebarriga* (page 140) can become pretty impassioned. Should you add the cilantro at the beginning or the end of cooking? Do you have to dice the plantain in the traditional way (with a thumbnail) or will a knife ruin the texture? Everyone has an opinion about how to cook the local dishes, and kitchen mentors like my Aunt Donna, her friend Clota Peña, my wife's mother and grandmother, and both of my parents have contributed immeasurably to the recipes in this book. Thankfully, all have strong feelings about the way the classic dishes of the Bogotanos should be cooked. (I've always been interested to note that recipes from other Colombian regions like Tolima or Cartagena are considered almost as foreign as American burgers or Italian pasta, both of which are popular in Bogotá.)

As the child of two hardworking parents, I spent a great deal of time prowling the streets of Bogotá with my friends. After school, we'd seek out the best place to find a hot grilled *arepa* stuffed with melting cheese, the bakery with the most tempting *bizcochos* (cookies) or the richest hot chocolate. The fruit and vegetable markets of Bogotá are dazzling in their variety: Like many children, I learned from my mother at a young age how to choose among the papayas, mangoes, moras, curubas, maracuyas, and countless other fruits that are the basis of Colombia's wonderful juices. (It's been entertaining to me to witness the current "smoothie" craze sweeping the States; in Colombia, fresh juices mixed with milk, water, or ice—called *batidas*—are as familiar as orange juice is in Florida.)

Weekends meant a large family gathering at home with lots of cooking—or, often, a long meal at one of the popular steakhouses in the mountains outside the city. These wonderful institutions boast huge open grills set atop flaming coals in the middle of the restaurant—and thick steaks marinated till tender, dark morcilla and chorizo sausages, and roasted *papas criollas,* the tiny yellow potatoes with an earthiness no American potato can replicate. Or we'd indulge in another Colombian tradition, the *picada:* platters of bite-size empanadas, cornmeal *arepas,* slices of fried plantain, and chunks of sausage eaten one after another, all dipped into the fiery, cilantro-infused hot sauce known as *ají.* Family trips to the port city of Cartagena and the lovely Caribbean islands of San Andrés always meant a chance to taste my favorite rice cooked in coconut, wonderful with grilled and fried fish prepared right on the beach. And if the grown-ups had had too much fun the night before—Colombians love their native anise brandy, known as *aguardiente*—we would all have *changua* for breakfast, a restorative and soothing soup of bread, milk, poached eggs, onions, and cilantro.

I have only just begun to explore the cuisine of my native country, much less the remainder of the continent. The foods that I grew up with are so irresistible that I'm proud to present them, in my own versions, as modern Latin American home cooking. But at age sixteen, when my training began with an apprenticeship with chef Larry Forgione at Brooklyn's River Café, I was just a kid looking for an after-school job, not an ambitious culinary professional. In that rigorous atmosphere, I quickly figured out that learning to cook "seriously" would mean learning classic French cuisine—and forgetting about my own cooking traditions when I was at work. It certainly didn't occur to me then that someday I might be known for an innovative synthesis of Latin, French, and Mediterranean cooking that has since become my signature cuisine. Instead, the River Café's dedication to seasonal and local ingredients began to teach me the principles of California-influenced New American cooking. I continued that learning process with chef Jonathan Waxman at the white-hot restaurant Jams in the 1980s.

I did make a stop in between to study the traditional French system of haute cuisine with celebrated chef Michel Guerard at Eugenie-les-Bains, a difficult but instructive experience. There was an enormous amount to be learned about flavors in that kitchen—how to layer them, contrast them, deepen them—and I was an eager nineteen-year-old sponge, soaking up all the information I could. It was exciting to be studying with the masters, but I didn't always learn what I was supposed to! Instead of acquiring a reverent, respectful attitude toward the French system of apprenticeship, I often rebelled against it. I believe that there are a lot of ways to be a great cook. However, my way doesn't require years of training to cut lemons, weeks passed in perfecting stocks, or months spent practicing with a pastry tube. It's about putting great flavor over perfect technique, following your taste instead of the rules, and choosing appealing dishes over impressive ones. The vibrant, simple, flavor-packed cuisine these "Palomino Principles" have led me to create is contained in the pages of this book.

In the early years, it was necessary for me to ignore my Colombian heritage—at least when I was in the kitchen. Only a few major U.S. chefs, like Santa Fe's Mark Miller and Miami's Steven Raichlen, had then begun to explore the culinary richness of Latin America and the Caribbean. The last ten years, of course, have seen a veritable explosion of interest in this area, especially in the flavor-rich Mexican and Cuban *cocinas*. Douglas Rodriguez, the pioneering chef at Yuca and Patria, has been a frequent inspiration, but his culinary orientation leans much more toward Cuba and the Caribbean than mine. Until I began to present the sophisticated and fascinating area of South American cooking in my restaurants Inca Grill and Bistro Latino, no New York chef had penetrated the vast and vastly misunderstood area beyond Mexico and the Caribbean. The luscious coconut-fish soups I had enjoyed on family trips to Cartagena, the tart ceviches of Peru, the deep-flavored caramelized milk desserts popular across the continent have been almost completely unknown outside their communities.

Now, after almost twenty years of cooking professionally, I bring a combination of Latin, European, and American heritage and influence to the kitchen. But today I am an

American chef first, so I celebrate them all. For example, in going beyond the Spanish connection between the Mediterranean and Latin America, I've synthesized new flavorings and textures with classic techniques and ingredients, and invented a truly new American cuisine that shines with big, sunny flavors.

Of course, the enormous influence of Spain is ever-present in my kitchen (as it is throughout South America), with contributions from bright gazpachos to fragrant *camarones al ajillo* to creamy flans. French bistro cooking, which takes home cooking rather than haute cuisine as its inspiration, relies on simple preparations like soups, stews, grills, and quick sautés—and so do I. These are dishes that don't require a lot of work or expertise, but glean lots of flavor from their ingredients. And most important to my cooking are the essential ingredients of the New World, the *Nuevo Mundo*—potatoes, peppers, corn, plantains, tomatoes, chiles, cilantro, avocados, and mangoes. To these I add the key flavorings of the Mediterranean—fruity olive oil, briny capers, garlic, lemon and lime juices, red wine, and pungent herbs and spices like thyme, saffron, and parsley.

That's how Bistro Latino was born—a synthesis of French and New American cooking with Mediterranean and New World flavors that is easy, interesting, and satisfying enough to eat every day. This collection of 150 recipes reflects how I cook in my restaurant kitchens, but also how I cook at home for my family. I've organized the recipes into chapters that reflect the way we eat in the States, which is a bit different from the Latin way. For example, empanadas (pages 72–77) and tamales are not only served as appetizers in Colombia but as lunch, late-night snacks, and even, occasionally, breakfast. The distinction between a soup and a stew is not very great: Most soups are thick enough to make a substantial lunch or light dinner, while most stews have plenty of delicious liquid to sop with fried plantains or rice. The largest meal is eaten at midday, while at night a fat *tamal* (page 138) or scrambled eggs with chorizo sausage on cornmeal *arepas* (page 47) might suffice. Raw vegetable salads are rare, but so are rich desserts: Fresh fruit usually appears at the table after lunch or dinner, while sweets are eaten in the afternoon. Hearty side dishes like red beans (page 172) or potatoes in a spicy cheese sauce (page 163) occasionally become entrees; some steak dishes appear only at breakfast time. As much as possible, I've tried to blend Latin, French, and American influences into courses and dishes that are recognizable to an American audience, but still fresh and appealing.

What always amazes me—and, I'm willing to bet, will excite you—is how easy it is to move between these cuisines. Classic Riviera bouillabaisse is instantly reinvented with red snapper fillets, a generous handful of fresh cilantro, and smoky chipotle puree (page 3). The lemony seafood salads that you find everywhere on the Mediterranean coastline appear in Peru and Colombia as no-cook ceviches infused with lime, tomato, and chile (pages 64–67). Mediterranean-rim cooks have always relied on the bounty of the sea for light, simple, intensely flavorful fish dishes; Peruvian, Colombian, and Chilean cooks, with their ready access to the sea, do the same.

For Bistro Latino, I have created a delectable seafood hash with fresh corn and chopped tomato (page 125), and added fresh cilantro to the classic Spanish *camarones al ajillo,* shrimp baked in lots of garlic and aromatic olive oil (page 70). Of course, peppery French *steak frites* is a close cousin to Argentine grilled steak with fried yuca and an aromatic *chimichurri* sauce, while a Provençal beef daube takes the form of oxtail slow-simmered in Chilean red wine with herbs, yuca, and potatoes (page 112). The strong African influence on the unique cuisine of Brazil shines in a creamy frozen chocolate pudding studded with crunchy toasted *caju*—or, as we know them better, cashew nuts (page 178). Fragrant Colombian coffee infuses my chocolate brownies (page 179), and tropical fruits bring bright flavors and colors to irresistible summertime fruit shakes.

With punchy ingredients like these, only the simplest preparations are wanted or needed, making Bistro Latino an ideal way for home cooks to explore the true flavors of Latin America. As you use this book, you may notice that I don't use a lot of exotic spices or hot chiles in my kitchen. Mexican cooking aside, most of Latin American cooking is lightly seasoned and rarely spicy. Flavor is more likely to come from a sprinkling of scallions, a fresh sauce, or a touch of nutty-sweet coconut milk and ripe tomato than from strong spices and hot peppers. The first chapter on Bistro Latino Basics will give you some of the tools you need to get started.

Soon, you'll see how the bright, clean tastes of fresh salmon and cilantro need only a squeeze of lemon to make a perfect, palate-teasing appetizer (page 63). Scallions and chorizo pack so much flavor that just the addition of delicate chicken breasts and creamy goat cheese leads to a perfectly balanced dish full of taste and texture contrasts (page 130). Flan, the ubiquitous South American custard (everyone from Rio to Tierra del Fuego swears that his mother's is the best) becomes lighter, brighter, and more tropical with a bit of passionfruit puree (page 184). And everyone loves classic Latin cocktails like Pisco Sours (page 53) and Brazil's formidable *Caipirinha* (page 54). Use the recipes that follow as a starting point for your Latin journey—your kitchen will never be quite the same.

# Bistro Latino Basics

# NOTES ON INGREDIENTS

## Beans

Dried beans are a near-universal Latin staple. Although most North American cookbooks call for presoaking and draining most types of beans, the simpler Latin method starts the cooking with dried beans and cold water. This is my method for the black, pink, and cranberry beans that are used in the following recipes:

Rinse and pick over the beans, then place in a large pot. Cover with cold water, bring to a simmer, and let simmer, covered, until the beans are softened but not mushy. This can take anywhere from 1 to 2 hours, depending on the size and age of the beans. Check the beans frequently to make sure they are covered with water; add more boiling water as needed. Make sure the mixture stays at a simmer; boiling will make the beans burst. To prevent toughening, add salt only toward the end of the cooking.

An exception to the "no presoaking" rule are garbanzos or chickpeas. These must be soaked in cold water to cover for at least 8 hours before cooking. After soaking, proceed as instructed above. Garbanzos can take as long as 2¼ hours to cook tender.

## Chipotle Puree

Chipotles are simply smoked jalapeño peppers, a staple of the Mexican kitchen. They are readily available here, canned in a sauce of vinegar and tomato and sold as *chipotles in adobo*. Pureed smooth, they make a marvelous paste that I could not get along without in my kitchen. Simply empty the contents of the can into a blender and process until smooth. One *chipotle in adobo* yields about 1 tablespoon puree.

## Chorizos

Chorizos, or pork sausages, are very popular and found in almost every Latin cuisine—but different cooks can mean very different things by the word *chorizo*. I use Colombian chorizo, which is lighter in color and less spicy than, say, Mexican chorizo. Chorizo comes two ways: fresh and dry. The fresh chorizo is soft, like an Italian sausage, and contains a mixture of beef, pork, salt, and herbs. Dry chorizo is a firmer, lightly smoked sausage that is cooked but still moist (not as hard as a pepperoni). In texture, dry chorizo is similar to kosher salami. It does not need to be cooked before using, although it can be heated or browned.

Many different chorizos are available in Latin markets, but using good-quality Italian sausage (preferably made with parsley) browned with a sprinkling of sazón Goya (page 6) as a substitute for fresh chorizo would be quite acceptable. The flavor will be different, but still good. Colombian dry chorizo is much milder than andouille or linguiça, but you can use them as substitutes if you like spice and garlic. Otherwise, kielbasa or a similar mild cooked sausage can be used.

## Coconut Milk/Coconut Cream

I use only unsweetened coconut milk in cooking. It's readily available canned in Latin, Indian, Caribbean, and Asian markets; shake well before using. I don't recommend experimenting with whole coconuts in a home kitchen, but if you're an experienced coconut milker, by all means substitute fresh coconut milk in these recipes.

Coconut cream is a sweetened, condensed coconut milk that is often used in desserts and drinks. Look for it with the drink mixers at your supermarket. The most common brand in the States seems to be Coco Lopez, and that's what I've used in testing the recipes.

## Crema Agria

Literally "sour cream," Latin *crema agria* is thinner and less sour than the product we know by that name. French crème fraîche or sour cream thinned with a little heavy cream can be substituted. To make your own from scratch: Combine two parts heavy cream and one part sour cream in a bowl. Mix well, cover with a clean kitchen towel, and leave out overnight at room temperature. When thickened, cover tightly with plastic wrap, and refrigerate until ready to use.

## Guava Paste

The most versatile form of the guava fruit is guava paste, also called guava jam. It is sold in Latin markets in boxes and cans and is a thick, dark orange fruit paste. I usually use it diced, which is easier to do if you chill the paste for 30 minutes beforehand.

## Olive Oil

I very rarely use extra-virgin olive oil in cooking, partly because it seems like an unnecessary luxury, but mostly because I don't like the strong taste it imparts to food. It's rarely used as a cooking medium in Latin America. I use a neutral-tasting pure-grade olive oil for sautéing; there are several on the market, often labeled as "light" olive oil. This isn't an official term, but a descriptive one. They are light in texture and flavor, which is what you want in the following recipes. Just make sure the oil you use doesn't have a strong acidic "bite."

# Panela

Much used as a sweetener throughout Latin America, *panela* is pure, hardened cane syrup, shaped into round loaves. Brown and brick-hard, it is found in Latin and Caribbean markets. Unlike our brown sugar, from which the molasses is first removed and then put back, *panela* is unrefined. In Colombia, *panela* is usually made into a syrup before using it as an ingredient, but it can simply be grated or chopped to a sugary texture. Dark brown sugar is a perfectly acceptable substitute, but it will not have quite as much toasty caramel flavor.

# Papas Criollas

*Papas criollas* are easily found in Latin markets, but most supermarkets will not have them. Tender, tiny, starchy yellow potatoes traditional in Colombia, they are pickled to preserve them for transport to the United States. They add strong potato flavor and a velvety texture to soups and stews. If you can't locate them at a Latin market, however, just use any small, starchy potatoes boiled soft in plenty of salted water.

# Plantains (Plátanos)

Now found everywhere in the States, plantains are a Latin staple. Bigger and starchier than bananas, they are useful and delicious at all stages of ripeness, from green to yellow to black. In the recipes that follow, I've specified "green" plantains, "ripe" plantains (yellow, with some blackening), or "very ripe" plantains (completely black, soft, and limp). I can't stress enough how important it is to use the plantains at the correct stage of ripeness: There are important differences in flavor and texture.

*To peel a green plantain,* put the whole plantain to soak in warm water for 20 minutes or so. Cut off both ends of the plantain and use the tip of a knife to cut two or three long slits in the skin from one end to the other. At this point, it is usually possible to open up the skin along the slits and peel it off with your hands. If not, simply peel with a small knife, as you would a potato.

Ripe and very ripe plantains can be peeled like bananas.

# Roasted Corn

Many of my recipes call for roasted corn. Whole ears of corn, left in the husks, can be oven-roasted at 375 degrees for 15 to 20 minutes. Remove the tough outer husks and the corn silk and place the ears directly on the oven rack. To achieve a somewhat similar effect with frozen corn kernels, toss with olive oil and a little garlic in a very hot skillet until dry and lightly browned.

## Roasted Garlic

I much prefer the less acidic and overpowering flavor of garlic that has been roasted before it is added to a dish. Since most of my recipes are quick-cooking, the garlic tastes best when partly cooked beforehand, hence the following technique. To make ¼ cup roasted garlic puree, peel 12 large garlic cloves and combine them with 1 tablespoon olive oil on a sheet of aluminum foil. Wrap tightly and bake in a preheated 350-degree oven until softened but not mushy or sweet, about 15 minutes. Puree with ¼ cup light-flavored olive oil, cover tightly, and use within one week.

## Roasted Peppers

I prefer the flavor of peppers roasted over an open flame. Skewer a whole pepper on the end of a long fork. Hold the pepper directly over a gas flame or over hot coals in a grill, turning to roast all the sides. When the skin is completely black and charred, transfer the pepper to a thick plastic or brown paper bag and close the top. When cool enough to handle, use your hands to gently pull out the stem and rub off the skin. Cut the pepper into quarters and use your hands to rub off the seeds. *Do not rinse the peppers, or you will lose all the flavorful oils.* Use immediately or cover with olive oil, cover tightly, and refrigerate for up to three days.

If you do not have a gas stove or grill, sear the skins of the peppers on a very hot griddle or in a cast-iron skillet, turning with tongs until black.

## Sazón Goya

Sazón Goya is available at supermarkets across the country. It's a spice blend that incorporates key Latin flavorings—mostly cumin and garlic—as well as monosodium glutamate. There are a few variations; I always use the one with cilantro and achiote, for color. One envelope contains 1½ teaspoons sazón. If you'd rather not use it, or can't find it, substitute an equal amount of the following spice blend:

**1 part annatto powder (ground achiote seeds),**
**available at Latin and Indian markets**
**2 parts ground cumin**
**2 parts garlic powder**
**1 part freshly ground black pepper**
**3 parts kosher salt**

# Sweetened Condensed Milk

Sweetened condensed milk is a mixture of whole milk and sugar, long familiar to both North and South American cooks. In South America, sweetened condensed milk usually goes through one more cooking stage before it is used: It is heated in the can until the sugar caramelizes, lending a toasty flavor and color to the thick milk. The resulting sweet goes under many names—*dulce de leche, arequipe, manjar blanco, cajeta,* and others. It is a quick and easy adaptation of a classic Spanish technique for slowly cooking down goat's, cow's, or even almond milk until a thick and creamy pudding forms. It can be a dessert on its own or an ingredient in cookies, cakes, muffins, or ice cream.

The caramelizing process is simple. Put the cans in a pot deep enough to hold water to cover the cans, cover with cool water, and bring to a boil over high heat. Once the water has come to a boil, boil for one hour and forty-five minutes to achieve the best flavor and color, adding more water as needed to keep the cans covered at all times. *Never boil the cans for more than two hours:* You then run the risk of having them explode, although this has never actually happened to me—and I've been using this technique since I was a little boy! Turn the cans occasionally to stir the milk. Let the cans cool to room temperature before opening.

If this approach doesn't appeal to you, you can caramelize milk from scratch. To do this, place 1 quart whole milk, 1 pound granulated sugar (2 cups), ¼ teaspoon baking soda, and a pinch of ground cinnamon in a large saucepan over medium heat for 15 to 20 minutes without stirring. Reduce the heat to low and cook, stirring constantly with a wooden spoon, for 25 to 30 minutes. When the mixture starts to get so thick you can see the bottom of the saucepan as you stir, remove from the heat and keep at room temperature (if it cools off too much, you may have to heat it to soften). This makes 2 cups of caramelized milk, the equivalent of two 8-ounce cans of condensed milk. Any extra you do not use will keep, covered, in the refrigerator for up to two weeks.

## Toasted Nuts

I always toast nuts before using them to bring out their flavor and natural toastiness. Spread whole or chopped nuts on a baking sheet and place in a preheated 350-degree oven. Check them after 3 minutes and shake the pan to ensure even browning. After that, check them every minute, and remove from the oven as soon as they are fragrant and golden brown. They will burn very quickly after this point; you may want to remove them from the baking sheet as soon as they come out of the oven if there is any hint of burning.

## Vinegar

At Bistro Latino, I usually use distilled white vinegar in the kitchen, which will sound a bit heretical to cooks who have always been told that it is "too harsh." That is sometimes true—in French cooking, for example, with its subtle flavors, white vinegar is overpowering. However, I've found that the clean taste and neutral tartness of white vinegar is best suited to the bold ingredients of my Latin food. White vinegar is almost always used in Latin American kitchens, so it is also a more authentic choice. If you don't have it in the house, white wine vinegar can be substituted—but you will need more to achieve the correct acidity.

## Yuca

Yuca is an unusual case of the frozen vegetable actually being preferable to the fresh. Yuca is very hard to peel and very tough; the freezing process breaks down the fibers, improving the texture. I always use it and recommend that you do too; it's available in freezer sections of most supermarkets and in Latin, Caribbean, and African markets, sometimes under the name of *cassava*. I prefer the Goya product, as it is cut into very large chunks.

To use in cooking, place the frozen yuca in a saucepan, cover with boiling water or a combination of water and stock (which greatly improves the flavor), and let simmer until soft all the way through, about 30 minutes. Because yuca is so starchy, it holds together even when cooked soft. Drain, pull or cut out the tough, stringy core, and dice the yuca as specified in the recipe.

## Fresh Hot Pepper Sauce (*Ají*)

Makes about 1½ cups

- 3 ripe plum tomatoes, seeded and cut into ¼-inch dice
- 1 tablespoon freshly squeezed lemon juice
- 1 teaspoon kosher salt
- 1 teaspoon Tabasco or other hot sauce, or more to taste
- 3 scallions, white and pale green parts, thinly sliced
- 2 tablespoons distilled white or red wine vinegar
- ¼ cup olive oil
- ½ cup chopped cilantro leaves

**A**jí is the fundamental Colombian hot sauce, used to spark up everything from my Tía Donna's Colombian Tamales (page 138) to *Papas Chorreadas* (page 162). Sweet, fiery Colombian *ají,* or hot peppers, are virtually impossible to get in this country. They possess a unique combination of fruitiness and heat. The punch of Tabasco works well as a substitute in this particular sauce, but you can also use a finely minced fresh chile of your choice. Habaneros have a lovely perfume, but beware: They're super-hot! The dominant flavors here should be refreshing cilantro and scallion, not chile heat.

**Combine all the ingredients** in a medium-size nonreactive bowl and whisk to combine. Use immediately or cover tightly and refrigerate up to two days. Mix well before serving.

# Fresh Hot Pepper Sauce with Avocado (*Aji Verde*)

Makes about 2 cups

**2 ripe Hass avocados, pitted, peeled, and diced**

**3 hard-boiled eggs, peeled**

**½ cup chopped cilantro leaves**

**2 scallions, white and pale green parts, thinly sliced**

**1 large ripe tomato, seeded and cut into ¼-inch dice**

**½ teaspoon Tabasco or other hot sauce, or more to taste**

**Freshly squeezed juice of ½ lemon**

This is a smoother, richer *aji*, thanks to the addition of ripe avocados and creamy egg yolks. The herbal notes of cilantro and the crunch of scallion are especially important here, so don't make it too far in advance. This is a must with my favorite Colombian Sirloin Empanadas (page 72).

**In a medium-size nonreactive bowl,** mash the avocados together with a fork. Coarsely grate the eggs into the bowl, add the remaining ingredients, and mix well. Use immediately or cover tightly and refrigerate up to 24 hours. Mix well before serving.

# Tomato-Onion Sauce (*Hogo*)

Makes about 1½ cups

**2 tablespoons olive oil**

**3 ripe medium-size tomatoes, seeded and cut into ¼-inch dice**

**1 small onion, chopped**

**1 teaspoon minced garlic**

**¾ teaspoon sazón Goya (page 6)**

**⅓ cup finely chopped scallions, white and pale green parts**

**⅓ cup chopped cilantro leaves**

**1 bay leaf**

**1 cup Chicken Stock (page 32), canned low-sodium chicken broth, or water**

**Kosher salt and freshly ground black pepper to taste**

*Hogo* is as fundamental to the Colombian kitchen as *sofrito* is to the Spanish one. It can be a sauce, relish, or cooking medium—and it is stirred into countless soups and stews to instantly deepen the flavors. A traditional *hogo* does not include garlic, but I can't resist adding it for the extra boost it gives to the tomato flavor. Use it in Colombian Red Beans (page 172) or in Aromatic Braised Oxtail with Yuca, Potatoes, and *Hogo* (page 112)—or cook some rice in *hogo* and stock for a savory side dish. *Hogo* can be reduced more or less, depending on how you plan to use it—thicker when used as a sauce, thinner when stirred into a soup or stew.

**In a medium-size nonreactive skillet,** heat the oil over medium heat. Add the remaining ingredients in order, stirring between additions. Simmer (reduce the heat if necessary), stirring occasionally, until the sauce reaches the desired consistency, 7 to 10 minutes. Use immediately or cover tightly and refrigerate up to one week. Mix well before serving.

# Argentine Green Sauce (*Chimichurri*)

Makes about 2 cups

**3 scallions, white and pale green parts, thinly sliced**

**2 tablespoons chopped fresh oregano leaves**

**3 tablespoons chopped fresh parsley leaves**

**2 tablespoons chopped cilantro leaves**

**½ cup distilled white or red wine vinegar**

**1 cup olive oil**

**1 teaspoon finely minced garlic**

**Freshly squeezed juice of 1 lemon**

**Kosher salt to taste**

More than any other country in South America, Argentina and its cuisine have been influenced by the Italian immigrants who flocked there in the nineteenth century. *Chimichurri* is a clear link between European and Latin cooking; it's very similar to the herbal Italian sauce for meat and fish known as *salsa verde*. *Chimichurri* uses cilantro instead of the capers that would be used in Italy to add the final green note that makes this piquant sauce so good on grilled steak or fried empanadas.

**Combine all the ingredients** in a medium-size nonreactive bowl and whisk to combine. Use immediately or cover tightly and refrigerate up to two days. Mix well before serving.

# Pineapple-Almond Salsa

Makes 3½ cups

1 cup whole almonds, toasted
   (page 8) and coarsely chopped

3 cups ½-inch peeled fresh pineapple
   dice

2 small shallots, minced

1 teaspoon peeled and grated fresh
   ginger

2 tablespoons chopped cilantro leaves

2 tablespoons olive oil

½ cup pineapple juice

1 teaspoon freshly squeezed lime juice,
   or more to taste

Kosher salt and freshly ground black
   pepper to taste

**F**irm whitefish like cod, flounder, and halibut benefit from the nuttiness of almonds and the sweet tang of fresh pineapple. This salsa is almost a salad. In a pinch, you can use canned pineapple.

**Combine all the ingredients** in a medium-size nonreactive bowl and mix to combine. Use immediately or cover tightly and refrigerate up to 24 hours. Mix well before serving.

# Citrus-Chipotle Salsa

*Makes about 1½ cups*

**4 peeled pink grapefruit segments, seeded and diced**

**3 peeled lemon segments, seeded and diced**

**5 peeled orange segments, seeded and diced**

**1 tablespoon light-flavored olive oil**

**1 teaspoon chipotle puree (page 3)**

**1 teaspoon chopped fresh mint leaves**

**Kosher salt and freshly ground black pepper to taste**

The richness of meaty fish like tuna and salmon is best savored with a perky salsa like this one. Try it with my Pan-Roasted Tuna Steaks with Crisp Yuca Crust (page 117). You can adjust the amounts of orange, lemon, and grapefruit to suit your taste. The key is to get rid of as much of the fruits' natural white pith and membrane as possible.

**In a medium-size nonreactive bowl,** toss the citrus pieces together. Add the remaining ingredients and mix to combine. Use immediately or cover tightly and refrigerate up to 24 hours. Mix well before serving.

# Chayote-Mango Salsa

Makes about 4 cups

**1 large chayote, peeled, pitted, and cut into ¼-inch dice**

**3 mangoes, peeled, pitted, and cut into ¼-inch dice**

**1 teaspoon peeled and grated fresh ginger**

**1 teaspoon chipotle puree (page 3)**

**1 tablespoon freshly squeezed lime juice**

**Kosher salt and freshly ground black pepper to taste**

Crisp, cool chayote and juicy, sweet mango make a fabulous salsa for pork, chicken, and grilled fish. This can also be served as a side salad.

**Combine all the ingredients** in a large nonreactive bowl and mix to combine. Use immediately or cover tightly and refrigerate up to 24 hours. Mix well before serving.

# Hot Papaya Salsa

Makes about 4 cups

**1½ cups seeded and diced red bell pepper**

**1½ cups peeled, seeded, and diced ripe papaya**

**½ cup minced fresh chives**

**¾ cup pineapple juice**

**1 teaspoon chipotle puree (page 3), or less to taste**

**1 large cucumber, peeled, seeded, and diced**

**Kosher salt and freshly ground black pepper to taste**

Many of the hot peppers used in the Colombian kitchen have a lot of natural sweetness as well as heat. Combining sweet fruit with red bell pepper and spicy chipotle creates a similar effect. The cool crunch of cucumber lightens the mixture. This is wonderful with grilled fish and chicken, especially meaty Marinated Tuna Steaks (page 147).

**Combine all the ingredients** in a medium-size nonreactive bowl and mix to combine. Use immediately or cover tightly and refrigerate up to 24 hours. Mix well before serving.

# Black Bean–
# Roasted Corn
# Salsa

*Makes about 4 cups*

**4 ears corn (do not remove the husks)**
**   or 2 cups frozen kernels**
**2 tablespoons olive oil**
**1 garlic clove, minced**
**2 cups drained freshly cooked**
**   (page 3) or canned black beans**
**4 ripe plum tomatoes, diced**
**¼ cup chopped cilantro leaves**

Somewhere between a salsa and a salad, this chunky mixture makes a great topping for grilled fish, chicken, and meat. It's the smokiness of the corn harmonizing with the flavor of the grill that does it.

**If using fresh corn,** preheat the oven to 375 degrees. Remove the tough outer husks and the corn silk. Place the ears directly on the oven rack and bake for 15 minutes. When cool enough to handle, husk the corn, cut the kernels from the cobs, and place in a medium-size nonreactive bowl. Add the oil and garlic and mix to combine.

If using frozen corn, heat the oil in a small skillet over high heat. Add the garlic and corn and cook, stirring, over high heat until the corn is browned. Transfer to a medium-size nonreactive bowl and set aside to cool.

Add the remaining ingredients and mix to combine. Serve at room temperature; do not refrigerate.

# Roasted Beet–
# Red Wine Sauce

Makes 3 cups

**1 tablespoon olive oil**

**½ medium-size red onion, chopped**

**2 medium-size beets, peeled and cut
    into ½-inch dice**

**½ cup dry red wine**

**¼ cup firmly packed *panela* (page 5)
    or dark brown sugar**

**7 cups water**

**Kosher salt and freshly ground black
    pepper to taste**

This easy but elegant sauce has deep color and deeper flavor. Serve with grilled salmon or tuna steak.

**In a medium-size heavy nonreactive saucepan,** heat the oil over medium heat. Add the onion and beets and cook, stirring, until softened, 5 to 8 minutes. Add the wine, bring to a simmer, and cook, stirring, until the liquid is reduced to a thick syrup. Add the sugar and 6 cups of the water, bring back to a simmer, and cook, stirring occasionally, until thick and syrupy, about 45 minutes. Add half of the remaining cup of water and blend with an immersion blender or in a blender until smooth. Season with salt and pepper. If desired, thin the sauce with the remaining ½ cup water. Serve immediately or cover tightly and refrigerate up to three days. Mix well before serving.

# Cilantro Pesto

*Makes about 2 cups*

**2 garlic cloves**

**2½ cups loosely packed cilantro leaves**

**¼ cup chopped fresh chives**

**½ teaspoon kosher salt**

**1 cup olive oil**

Heaven for cilantro lovers like me. This is actually much lighter than a pesto, since it contains neither cheese nor pine nuts—just plenty of fresh herb flavor. It does lose color quickly, but the flavor will remain.

**Combine all the ingredients** in a blender and process until smooth. Serve immediately or cover tightly and refrigerate up to two days. Mix well before serving.

# Braised Garlic-Thyme *Mojo* with Lime

Makes 1½ cups

½ teaspoon roasted garlic (page 6)

1 teaspoon chopped fresh oregano leaves

2 teaspoons chopped fresh thyme leaves

1½ cups Chicken Stock (page 32) or canned low-sodium chicken broth

Freshly squeezed juice of 1 lime

Kosher salt and freshly ground black pepper to taste

1 teaspoon cold unsalted butter

This *mojo (mojos* are generally thinner than salsas and can be used as marinades or as sauces) is my version of a Cuban classic. I love it drizzled on sliced steak.

**Combine the garlic,** oregano, thyme, stock, and lime juice in a small nonreactive saucepan and bring to a simmer. Let simmer for 5 minutes. Season with salt and pepper. Just before serving, whisk the butter into the hot sauce. Serve immediately.

# Mango Barbecue Sauce

Makes about 4 cups

1 small red onion, minced

1 tablespoon olive oil

4 cups mango juice or nectar

2 tablespoons chopped cilantro leaves

2 poblano chiles, roasted, peeled, and seeded (page 6)

Kosher salt and freshly ground black pepper to taste

This is a marvelous marinade or basting sauce. Slather a whole chicken with this sweet-hot, slightly smoky mixture before roasting for a savory glaze and tender meat, use it to coat a pork loin as it roasts, or to baste grilling tuna or salmon. Mango juice is available in boxes and jars at Caribbean, Indian, Latin, and Middle Eastern food shops; either is acceptable.

**In a medium-size nonreactive bowl,** whisk all the ingredients together. Let stand for 30 minutes before using to let the flavors blend. Use immediately or cover tightly and refrigerate up to one week. Mix well before serving.

# Chipotle-Guava Glaze

Makes 3 cups

1 tablespoon olive oil

1 tablespoon chopped fresh mint leaves

1 tablespoon chipotle puree (page 3)

1 tablespoon Dijon mustard

2 cups Chicken Stock (page 32) or
   canned low-sodium chicken broth

1 tablespoon firmly packed *panela*
   (page 5) or dark brown sugar

2½ cups fresh guava puree or thawed
   frozen guava pulp, pureed

Freshly squeezed juice of 2 limes, or
   more to taste

*T*he sweet smokiness of chipotle is a natural in a glaze. With mustard and brown sugar, this haunting sauce achieves a complex flavor. Brush it on grilling fish or chicken, or use in Garlic Shrimp and Pineapple Skewers (page 145).

**Combine all the ingredients** in a medium-size non-reactive saucepan, bring to a simmer, and let simmer until thickened and syrupy, about 20 minutes. Let cool to room temperature. Use immediately or cover tightly and refrigerate up to one week. Mix well before serving.

# Mango Vinaigrette

*Makes about 3 cups*

**2 medium-size shallots, minced**

**2½ cups mango juice or nectar**

**2 tablespoons chopped cilantro leaves**

**¼ cup white wine vinegar**

**½ cup vegetable oil**

**Kosher salt and freshly ground black pepper to taste**

Sweet mango, pungent shallots, and tangy vinegar combine to dramatically accent any tangle of greens. Crunchy ones like romaine and frisée are best, as this is a strong rather than subtle dressing. It's also very good on grilled seafood such as swordfish or as a dipping sauce for fat grilled shrimp. Mango juice is available in boxes and jars in Latin, Caribbean, Middle Eastern, and Indian markets.

**In a medium-size nonreactive bowl,** combine the shallots, mango juice, cilantro, and vinegar. Gradually whisk in the oil. Season with salt and pepper. Use immediately or cover tightly and refrigerate up to one week. Whisk or shake well before serving.

# Orange Vinaigrette

Makes about 1½ cups

1½ cups freshly squeezed orange juice

½ medium-size shallot, minced

¾ cup olive oil

Kosher salt and freshly ground black
  pepper to taste

A perennial favorite at Bistro Latino, this recipe replaces the usual vinegar in salad dressing with a reduction of fresh orange juice. It's as tangy as the original, but with a bit more sweetness and fragrance.

**In a small nonreactive saucepan,** simmer the orange juice until it is reduced by half. Let cool. In a medium-size nonreactive bowl, combine the reduced orange juice and shallot. Gradually whisk in the oil. Season with salt and pepper. Use immediately or cover tightly and refrigerate up to one week. Whisk or shake well before serving.

# Black Bean Vinaigrette

Makes about 1½ cups

1 cup drained freshly cooked (page 3)
   or canned black beans

1 teaspoon roasted garlic (page 6)

½ cup olive oil

1 teaspoon finely chopped cilantro
   leaves

3 tablespoons distilled white vinegar

Kosher salt and freshly ground black
   pepper to taste

Try this on roasted potatoes for a stunning Bistro Latino–style potato salad. In fact, it's good on any roasted or grilled vegetables.

**Combine all the ingredients** in a blender or food processor and process until smooth. Use immediately or cover tightly and refrigerate up to one week. Whisk or shake well before serving.

# Roasted Corn Vinaigrette

*Makes about 3 cups*

**3 ears fresh corn, roasted (page 5)
and kernels cut from the cobs**

**¾ cup white wine vinegar**

**1 small shallot, minced**

**1 tablespoon chopped cilantro leaves**

**1½ cups olive oil**

**Kosher salt and freshly ground black
pepper to taste**

Potatoes, squash, and beans—all New World ingredients—have a natural affinity for native American corn. When snappy shallots and fragrant cilantro are added to a vinaigrette with roasted corn, the result is fabulous on potato salad, baked squash, or black beans.

**Place the roasted corn kernels** in a food processor or blender. Add the vinegar, shallot, and cilantro and process until smooth. Gradually add the oil, blending until smooth. Season with salt and pepper. Use immediately or cover and refrigerate up to one week. Whisk or shake well before serving.

# Roasted Red Onion Vinaigrette

The sharpness of raw onion turns to smoky sweetness in a hot oven, making this a great way to add onion flavor to a salad without overpowering it.

Makes ¾ cup

1 large red onion, halved (do not peel)

½ cup extra-virgin olive oil

3 tablespoons white wine vinegar

1 tablespoon balsamic vinegar

Kosher salt and freshly ground black
pepper to taste

**Preheat the oven** to 375 degrees. Place the onion halves, cut side up, on a cookie sheet and bake for 15 minutes. Remove from the oven, peel off and discard the charred outer layer, and place the onion in a blender or food processor. Add the remaining ingredients and process until smooth. Use immediately or cover tightly and refrigerate up to one week. Whisk or shake well before serving.

# Tomato-Thyme Vinaigrette

Makes 1½ cups

1 cup extra-virgin olive oil

3 ripe plum tomatoes, cored and
    quartered lengthwise

1 garlic clove, minced

½ teaspoon chopped fresh thyme
    leaves

1 teaspoon chipotle puree (page 3)

¼ cup balsamic vinegar, or more to
    taste

Don't just put dressing on your vegetables—put vegetables in your dressing with this sweet, tart, spicy dressing, especially good on bean- and grain-based salads like my Chorizo, Artichoke, and Three-Bean Salad (page 84).

**In a medium-size nonreactive skillet,** heat the oil over medium-high heat. Add the tomatoes and cook, stirring, until softened. Add the remaining ingredients and cook, stirring, for 2 minutes. Let cool, transfer to a blender or food processor, and process until smooth. Use immediately or cover tightly and refrigerate up to one week. Whisk or shake well before serving.

# Cilantro Oil

*Makes about 1½ cups*

**1 tablespoon roasted garlic (page 6)**

**1 cup extra-virgin olive oil**

**1¼ cups chopped cilantro leaves**

**Kosher salt and freshly ground black
   pepper to taste**

Olive oil infused with cilantro has a multitude of uses in my kitchen—and it will in yours. Add it to salad dressings and marinades, or just drizzle on cooked fish, vegetables, pork, beef, and lamb; like parsley, cilantro brightens the flavors of almost anything you can think of.

**Place all the ingredients** in a blender or food processor and process until smooth. Use immediately or cover tightly and refrigerate up to three days. Whisk or shake well before serving.

# Chipotle Mayonnaise

*Makes about 1½ cups*

**2 large egg yolks, at room temperature**

**2 teaspoons chipotle puree (page 3)**

**1 tablespoon freshly squeezed lime juice, or more to taste**

**1 tablespoon white wine vinegar**

**½ teaspoon kosher salt**

**1 cup light-flavored olive oil, canola oil, or a combination**

Plain mayonnaise can be bland to some tastes, but with the irresistible warmth of chipotle added, this commonplace sauce reaches new heights of flavor. Chipotles are simply smoked jalapeño peppers; the smoking process transforms the flavors completely. They are available dried, but I usually use the plump, soft ones canned in a fiery sauce of vinegar and tomato called *adobo*. Chipotles are not used in the Colombian kitchen, but they are one of my favorite ingredients from the Mexican pantry. Lime provides the perfect cool, citric counterbalance in this easy sauce.

As always when you are going to consume raw eggs, make sure that you buy them from a reliable store with a good turnover—never from a farmstand—otherwise salmonella could be a problem. Always keep the mayonnaise refrigerated, and discard leftovers after two days.

**Combine the egg yolks,** chipotle puree, lime juice, vinegar, and salt in a food processor and process until thick and smooth. With the machine running, add the oil in a very thin stream; the mixture will become thick and stiff. Blend just until incorporated. Adjust the seasonings with lime juice, vinegar, and salt. Transfer to a nonreactive bowl, cover tightly and refrigerate at least one hour or up to two days. Discard after two days.

# Citrus Mayonnaise

Makes about 3 cups

**2 cups orange juice, preferably freshly squeezed**

**2 teaspoons freshly squeezed lime juice**

**2¼ cups vegetable oil**

**Up to 2 teaspoons white wine vinegar**

**Kosher salt to taste**

*T*raditional mayonnaise recipes call for lemon juice to balance the richness of the oil, but I love the fragrance of orange. Properly used, orange doesn't make the sauce sweet, but it does make it delicious. This is an egg-free mayonnaise, so you can keep it in the refrigerator as long as you like; if it "breaks," whisk it well or whirl it in a blender to restore the texture.

**In a small nonreactive saucepan,** simmer the orange juice until it is thick and syrupy and reduced to about ⅓ cup. Set aside until cool. Transfer to a blender or food processor and add 1 teaspoon lime juice. With the motor running, pour in 1 cup of the oil in a very thin stream. Repeat with the remaining teaspoon lime juice and the remaining 1¼ cups oil. Process until thick and well combined. Taste the mixture and adjust the seasonings with vinegar and salt. Transfer to a nonreactive bowl, cover tightly, and refrigerate at least one hour or up to one week.

# Chicken Stock

Makes about 1½ quarts (6 cups)

1 small fresh chicken, quartered

2½ quarts cold water, preferably
   filtered or spring

1 teaspoon kosher salt

1 large celery stalk with leaves,
   coarsely chopped

2 medium-size carrots, coarsely
   chopped

1 medium-size onion, coarsely chopped

1 bay leaf

1 bunch cilantro, roots discarded,
   washed

1 small head garlic, broken up into
   cloves

**Combine the chicken,** water, and salt in a stockpot and bring to a boil. Skim off any scum that rises to the surface. Reduce the heat to a simmer and add the remaining ingredients. Simmer for 1½ hours, skimming as necessary. Strain through a fine-mesh strainer into another pot or several containers, let cool, and refrigerate up to four days. Or pour into ice-cube trays and keep frozen up to two months.

# Fish Stock

*Makes about 2 quarts (8 cups)*

**2 tablespoons extra-virgin olive oil**

**2 medium-size red onions, coarsely chopped**

**2 ripe plum tomatoes, diced**

**1 bay leaf**

**1 large celery stalk with leaves, coarsely chopped**

**1 bunch cilantro, roots discarded, washed**

**1 head garlic, broken up into cloves**

**½ cup brandy**

**3 cups dry, light white wine such as Pinot Grigio**

**3 quarts cold water, preferably filtered or spring**

**3 pounds bones of red snapper or another mild, white-fleshed fish such as cod, halibut, sea bass, or flounder (available at your local fish store)**

**2 teaspoons kosher salt**

**In a stockpot,** heat the oil over medium heat. Add the onions, tomatoes, bay leaf, celery, cilantro, and garlic. Cook, stirring, until softened, 5 to 8 minutes. Do not let the vegetables brown. Add the brandy and stir. Add the wine, water, fish bones, and salt and bring to a boil. Reduce the heat to medium and simmer for 45 minutes to 1 hour, skimming off any surface foam as necessary. Strain through a fine-mesh strainer into another pot or several containers, let cool, and refrigerate up to four days. Or pour into ice-cube trays and keep frozen up to two months.

# Vegetable Stock

Makes about 2 quarts (8 cups)

1 large carrot, coarsely chopped

2 celery stalks with leaves, coarsely
   chopped

1 medium-size red onion, coarsely
   chopped

1 bay leaf

1 small bunch cilantro, roots discarded,
   washed

1 ear fresh corn, husked and cut into
   quarters, or ½ cup frozen corn
   kernels

1 teaspoon black peppercorns

1½ teaspoons kosher salt

3 quarts cold water, preferably filtered
   or spring

**Combine all the ingredients** in a stockpot and bring to a boil. Reduce the heat and simmer for 45 minutes, skimming off any surface foam as necessary. Strain into another pot or several containers, let cool, and refrigerate up to four days. Or pour into ice-cube trays and keep frozen up to two months.

# Arepas, Muffins, and Sandwiches

Cheese *Arepas*

Honey-Chipotle *Arepas*

Black Bean–Cumin *Arepas*

Shrimp *Arepas*

Colombian Cheese Biscuits (*Almojábanas*)

Brazilian Cheese-Yuca Bread (*Pan de Queso de Brasil*)

Plantain-Raisin Muffins

Guava Muffins (*Bizcochos de Gloria*)

Cuban Sandwich

Argentinaburger

Scrambled Eggs with Chorizo on *Arepas*

Chicken-Avocado Salad on *Arepas*

Vegetable-Stuffed *Arepas*

## Cheese Arepas

*Makes 8 large arepas*

**2 cups fine-ground white or yellow
   cornmeal**

**2 teaspoons kosher salt**

**3 tablespoons unsalted butter, melted**

**2 cups boiling water**

**3 tablespoons grated mozzarella
   cheese**

**Vegetable oil**

*A*repas, soft biscuits made from cornmeal, are often the very first food we Colombians eat: Teething babies chew on them all day long. They are a daily staple, served with coffee at breakfast or alongside meat and rice and beans for lunch and dinner. The first time I tasted Italian *polenta,* there was an immediate connection—a strong corn taste enhanced with butter, salt, and cheese.

As you can see, I couldn't stop there in terms of seasonings. The honey-chipotle variation is truly wonderful, judging by how fast they disappear from breadbaskets at Bistro Latino. With black beans and cumin added, *arepas* make a hearty meal out of a stew or chili. *Arepas* can be almost any size: These are quite large, about three inches across and a half inch thick. If you prefer smaller *arepas,* that's fine (smaller ones can be deep-fried instead of browned on a griddle). They should be about one and a half inches across and a half inch thick.

**In a large bowl,** combine the cornmeal and salt. Add the melted butter and boiling water and mix until smooth. The dough should be soft and a bit sticky; add more water or cornmeal if necessary. Add the mozzarella, mix well, and let rest for 15 minutes.

Divide the mixture into eight equal parts and roll each into a ball with your hands. Put the balls on a clean surface, cover with plastic wrap, and gently press down on each to flatten to a half inch thick. (The *arepas* can be made up to this point one day ahead and refrigerated. Bring them to room temperature before the final cooking.)

Heat a large griddle or a nonstick or cast-iron skillet over medium-high heat. Grease very lightly with oil and, working in batches if necessary, cook the *arepas* on both sides just until golden brown. Serve immediately.

# Honey-Chipotle Arepas

*Makes 8 large arepas*

**2 cups fine-ground white or yellow cornmeal**

**1 teaspoon kosher salt**

**2 cups boiling water**

**2 tablespoons olive oil**

**2 tablespoons honey**

**1 tablespoon chipotle puree (page 3)**

**Vegetable oil**

**In a large bowl,** combine the cornmeal and salt. Add the water, olive oil, honey, and chipotle puree and mix until smooth. The dough should be soft and a bit sticky; add more water or cornmeal if necessary. Let rest for 15 minutes.

Divide the mixture into eight equal parts and roll each into a ball with your hands. Put the balls on a clean surface, cover with plastic wrap, and gently press down on each to flatten to a half inch thick. (The *arepas* can be made up to this point one day ahead and refrigerated. Bring them to room temperature before the final cooking.)

Heat a large griddle or a nonstick or cast-iron skillet over medium-high heat. Grease very lightly with vegetable oil and, working in batches if necessary, cook the *arepas* on both sides just until golden brown. Serve immediately.

# Black Bean–Cumin Arepas

*Makes 16 medium-size arepas*

**2¼ cups Chicken Stock (page 32),**
**Vegetable Stock (page 34), or**
**canned low-sodium broth**

**2 cups fine-ground white or yellow**
**cornmeal**

**2 cups drained, cooked (page 3), or**
**canned black beans, mashed**

**1 teaspoon ground cumin**

**Kosher salt and freshly ground black**
**pepper to taste**

**Vegetable oil**

**Heat the stock** to a simmer in a small saucepan. Turn off the heat and let cool just until you can touch it.

Place the cornmeal in a large bowl and add most of the stock, the beans, and cumin and mix well. The dough should be soft and a bit sticky; add more stock or cornmeal if necessary. Season with salt and pepper and let rest for 15 minutes.

Divide the mixture into sixteen equal parts and roll each into a ball with your hands. Put the balls on a clean surface, cover with plastic wrap, and gently press down on each to flatten to a half inch thick. (The *arepas* can be made up to this point one day ahead and refrigerated. Bring them to room temperature before the final cooking.)

Heat a large griddle or a nonstick or cast-iron skillet over medium-high heat. Grease very lightly with vegetable oil and, working in batches if necessary, cook the *arepas* on both sides just until golden brown. Serve immediately.

This recipe combines the sunny taste of cornmeal with Latin ingredients like shrimp, onion, tomato, and cilantro for a bright summer dinner or brunch dish. Serve these instead of crabcakes, sit back, and collect the compliments.

## Shrimp Arepas

*Makes 12 arepas*

**4 large shrimp in their shells**

**3 tablespoons olive oil**

**3 cups water**

**1 medium-size onion, cut into small dice**

**4 ripe plum tomatoes, seeded and diced**

**1 cup coarsely chopped cilantro leaves**

**¾ teaspoon sazón Goya (page 6)**

**2 cups fine-ground white or yellow cornmeal**

**2 tablespoons shredded white cheddar cheese**

**Kosher salt and freshly ground black pepper to taste**

**Vegetable oil**

**Peel the raw shrimp,** reserving the shells, and set the shrimp aside. In a medium-size saucepan, heat 1 tablespoon of the olive oil over medium-high heat and cook the shrimp shells, stirring, about 3 minutes. Add the water and simmer, uncovered, until reduced to about 2 cups. Strain out the shells and keep the stock hot.

Slice the shrimp into ½-inch lengths. In a small skillet, heat the remaining 2 tablespoons oil over medium-high heat. Add the onion, tomatoes, shrimp, cilantro, and sazón and cook, stirring, until the shrimp are cooked through, 3 to 5 minutes.

In a large bowl, combine the cornmeal, cheese, hot stock, and tomato-onion-shrimp mixture. Mix thoroughly and season with salt and pepper. The dough should be soft and a bit sticky; add more cornmeal or hot water if necessary. Divide the mixture into twelve equal parts and roll each into a ball with your hands. Put the balls on a clean surface, cover with plastic wrap, and gently press down on each to flatten to a half inch thick. (The *arepas* can be made up to this point one day ahead and refrigerated. Bring them to room temperature before the final cooking.)

Heat a large griddle or a nonstick or cast-iron skillet over medium-high heat. Grease very lightly with oil and, working in batches if necessary, cook the *arepas* on both sides just until golden brown. Serve immediately.

# Colombian Cheese Biscuits (*Almojábanas*)

Makes about 18 small biscuits

**1 cup fresh whole-milk ricotta cheese**

**2 large eggs**

**2 cups all-purpose flour**

**1 teaspoon baking powder**

**½ teaspoon kosher salt**

**2 teaspoons granulated sugar**

These crumbly muffins are extraordinarily versatile—they're great with coffee for breakfast, with soup for lunch, or in the breadbasket at dinnertime. The cheese improves both the flavor and texture.

**In a large bowl,** combine the cheese, eggs, and flour and mix well with a sturdy whisk. Cover with a damp kitchen towel and let rest at room temperature for 2 hours. Add the remaining ingredients, mix well, and let rest at room temperature an additional 30 minutes.

Preheat the oven to 400 degrees. Lightly grease a baking sheet. With your hands, shape the dough into 1-inch balls and place on the sheet, pressing down lightly to flatten the bottoms. Bake until golden, 12 to 15 minutes. Let cool briefly on wire racks before serving.

## Brazilian Cheese-Yuca Bread (*Pan de Queso de Brasil*)

*Makes about 24 biscuits*

**½ cup vegetable oil**

**½ cup whole or 2% milk**

**1½ tablespoons butter, melted**

**3 large eggs**

**1 pound yuca flour**

**5 ounces white cheddar cheese, shredded**

**5 ounces yellow cheddar cheese, shredded**

**8 ounces Romano cheese, grated**

*assava* in both its sweet and bitter forms (the sweet kind is the vegetable known in Spanish-speaking Latin America as yuca) is tremendously important in the cuisine of Brazil. Bitter *cassava* is fatally poisonous in its raw state—but the resourceful women of the Amazon Basin long ago developed a way to peel, grate, and extract the poisonous juices from the huge tubers. *Manioc* is the Brazilian word for sweet *cassava,* the source for the flour used in this recipe. You can find yuca flour in boxes at any Caribbean or Latin market.

**In a large bowl,** combine the oil, milk, and butter and mix well. Mix in the eggs, then gradually stir in the flour. Cover with a damp kitchen towel and let rest at room temperature for 45 minutes.

Preheat the oven to 400 degrees. Lightly grease a baking sheet.

Add the cheeses to the bowl and mix well. With your hands, shape the dough into 1-inch balls and place on the sheet, pressing down lightly to flatten the bottoms. Bake until golden, 12 to 15 minutes. Let cool briefly on wire racks before serving.

# Plantain-Raisin Muffins

Makes 24 muffins

4 cups all-purpose flour

3½ cups sugar

1 tablespoon ground cinnamon

1 tablespoon ground nutmeg

2 teaspoons baking soda

1 teaspoon kosher salt

6 large eggs, lightly beaten

3 cups peanut oil

6 tablespoons guava paste (page 4), diced

4 large, very ripe plantains, peeled (page 5) and pureed in a food processor

1 cup raisins

Somewhere between a breakfast muffin and a robust dinner roll, these moist muffins are particularly long-lasting because of the plantains in them. That's why this recipe is for a very large batch, but you can certainly halve it if you like. Very ripe plantains (called *maduros,* or mature) are frequently used in baking in Colombia to add moisture and texture.

**Preheat the oven** to 350 degrees. In a large bowl, combine the flour, sugar, cinnamon, nutmeg, baking soda, and salt. Add the eggs, oil, and guava paste and mix until smooth. Add the plantain puree and mix to combine. Add the raisins and mix to combine.

Grease one or two large muffin tins, or line the cups with paper liners. Stir the batter, then use a ladle to fill each muffin cup three quarters full. Bake until puffy and browned, 25 to 30 minutes. Let cool on wire racks before serving.

# Guava Muffins (*Bizcochos de Gloria*)

Makes 6 to 8 large muffins

**Two 8-ounce cans sweetened condensed milk (do not open)**

**5 tablespoons sugar**

**3 tablespoons unsalted butter, at room temperature**

**5 large eggs**

**2 cups all-purpose flour**

**1 teaspoon baking powder**

**1 teaspoon kosher salt**

**1 tablespoon white wine**

**1 cup diced guava paste (page 4)**

In the nineteenth century, the gentility of Bogotá were famously fond of the habit of afternoon coffee and pastries. Coffee had recently replaced the more traditional drink of *panela* (hot sugar water), and cafés competed by inventing new cakes to lure customers. These days, few people slow down enough to eat *bizcochos* (small cakes and cookies), *postres* (sweets and pastries), or *tortas* (cakes) in the afternoon, but the legacy of those great days of baking remains in recipes like this one. To serve it as a dessert, split the muffins crosswise, place a scoop of ice cream on the bottom half, and replace the top of the muffin on the ice cream.

**Preheat the oven** to 350 degrees. Caramelize the milk according to the instructions on page 7. In a large bowl, beat the sugar and butter together until fluffy. Add the eggs and mix to combine. Sift the flour into another bowl and combine with the baking powder and salt. Stir the dry ingredients into the wet, then add the wine and mix until smooth.

Prepare a large muffin tin by greasing six of the cups or lining them with paper liners. Fill each cup one quarter full with muffin batter. Open the cans of condensed milk and spoon 2 tablespoons of caramelized milk on top of the batter. Sprinkle a few pieces of guava paste on top. Repeat two more times to create the layers, until each cup is three quarters full. If there are leftover ingredients, repeat in additional greased or lined muffin cups until they are used up. Bake until risen and golden, 25 to 30 minutes. Serve immediately or let cool on wire racks.

# Cuban Sandwich

*Makes 4 sandwiches*

**Unsalted butter as needed**

**Four 8-inch-long pieces French bread,**
**halved lengthwise**

**1 tablespoon Dijon mustard**

**8 thin slices roast pork**

**8 thin slices Westphalian or other**
**smoked ham**

**4 thin slices Swiss cheese**

**1 large dill pickle, thinly sliced**
**lengthwise into long, flat slices**

When I moved to Queens from Bogotá in my teens, this sandwich quickly became my favorite after-school and late-night snack. It was surprising to encounter the Latin cuisines I had never experienced in Latin America—Peruvian, Dominican, Puerto Rican, and Argentinian, to name a few—in my new home of New York City. This sandwich, though, knows no ethnic boundaries—everyone loves it. Sliced roast pork is available at any good deli counter.

**Heat a large griddle** or cast-iron skillet over high heat. Butter both halves of the breads, then spread the mustard on the top halves. On the bottom halves, layer two slices pork, two slices ham, one slice cheese, and one slice pickle. Place the top halves on top, then wrap tightly in a sheet of aluminum foil. Place the sandwiches on the griddle or skillet, then place another heavy skillet on top, resting the weight evenly over the sandwiches. (Or use a brick on top of each sandwich as a weight.) Cook for 3 to 5 minutes, pressing down occasionally to compress the sandwiches. Serve immediately.

# Argentinaburger

Makes 6 burgers

**3 pounds lean ground beef**

**¾ cup *Chimichurri* (page 12)**

**6 crusty round sandwich rolls, split and toasted if desired**

*N*ot a traditional Argentine dish but my own invention—a respectful tribute to the brilliant combination of rich beef and herbal, tart *chimichurri* sauce that is a national passion in Argentina. Eat these burgers with Purple Potato and Scallion Salad (page 88) and ripe avocado and tomato slices alongside for a perfect Bistro Latino family barbecue.

**In a large bowl,** combine the beef and *chimichurri* and mix well. Divide into six equal parts and shape into burgers. Refrigerate until ready to cook.

Heat a large cast-iron or other heavy skillet over medium-high heat or heat an outdoor grill to very hot. Cook the burgers to desired doneness and serve on rolls.

Fresh Salmon Tartare (page 63) and Goat Cheese and Basil Tamales (page 78)

Warm Shrimp, Cucumber, and Avocado Salad (page 83) on a Cheese *Arepa* (page 37) and
Fruit Gazpacho (page 100)

Ecuadoran Mixed Seafood Ceviche (page 65) with, left to right, Passionfruit *Batida* (page 55), Pisco Sour (page 53), and Brazilian Lime Cocktail *(Caipirinha)* (page 54)

Quick Chicken Stew with Corn (page 108)

Pan-Roasted Red Snapper with Garbanzos and Greens (page 120) and Colombian Potatoes
with Salt and Scallions (page 161)

Garlic Shrimp and Pineapple Skewers (page 145) and Roasted Corn and Garlic Rice (page 169)

Barbecued Ribs with Citrus Marmalade (page 148)

Caramelized *Arequipe* Cheesecake (page 180) and Mango Sorbet (a variation of Blackberry Sorbet, page 191) and Fried *Churros* with Berry Sauce (page 188)

# Scrambled Eggs with Chorizo on Arepas

This Palomino family brunch favorite is typical of the food Colombian-Americans tend to cook at home—Latin spice and spark grafted onto American home cooking. Instead of plain scrambled eggs, sausage, and toast for Sunday breakfast, try this more vibrant combination.

Makes 4 servings

1 tablespoon vegetable oil

1 fresh chorizo (page 3)

1 large ripe tomato, seeded and diced

3 scallions, white and pale green parts, thinly sliced

6 large eggs

Kosher salt and freshly ground black pepper to taste

4 large Cheese *Arepas* (page 37) or toasted English muffins

**Put the oil in** a medium-size nonreactive skillet. Remove the casing from the chorizo and crumble it into the skillet in very small pieces. Scatter the tomato and scallions over the chorizo and turn on the heat to medium-high. Cook, stirring occasionally, until the meat is lightly browned and some of the fat is rendered.

Meanwhile, beat the eggs in a medium-size bowl. Pour into the skillet, reduce the heat to medium-low, and cook, stirring constantly to make sure the eggs do not stick. Cook until firm but not dry. Season with salt and pepper and serve on top of *arepas* or English muffins.

# Chicken-Avocado Salad on *Arepas*

Makes 6 servings

**2 whole chicken breasts, preferably free range, with skin, on the bone**

**2 to 3 cups water, as needed**

**1 tablespoon kosher salt**

**1 bay leaf**

**2 ripe Hass avocados, peeled, pitted, and cut into ½-inch dice**

**2 scallions (optional), white and pale green parts, thinly sliced**

**2 tablespoons Chipotle Mayonnaise (page 30), or more to taste**

**2 teaspoons distilled white vinegar or fresh lemon juice, or more to taste**

**Kosher salt and freshly ground black pepper to taste**

**6 large Cheese *Arepas* (optional; page 37)**

I can never resist toying with American classics like chicken and potato salads, keeping them recognizable but adding flavor twists to make them interesting. Mixing in chipotle-infused mayonnaise and scallions instead of plain mayonnaise and the usual celery makes all the difference. Don't mix the ingredients together too far in advance, as the avocado will start to disintegrate. These knife-and-fork sandwiches make a great summer lunch with tart, spicy-sweet Fruit Gazpacho (page 100).

**In a large saucepan,** combine the chicken, water to barely cover, salt, and bay leaf. Bring to a boil, reduce to a simmer, and cover. Simmer gently until the chicken is firm, 35 to 45 minutes. Remove the chicken from the liquid and set aside to cool to room temperature, then refrigerate. Reserve the broth for another use.

When the chicken is cool, remove and discard the bone and skin. Cut or tear the meat into ½-inch pieces and place in a mixing bowl. Add the remaining salad ingredients (reserve the *arepas*), season with salt and pepper, and mix well. Slice the *arepas* horizontally in half, as you would an English muffin. Place the chicken salad on the bottom halves and set the tops on the filling. Serve immediately.

# Vegetable-Stuffed Arepas

Makes 4 servings

**3 tablespoons olive oil**

**2 teaspoons minced shallots**

**2 teaspoons minced garlic**

**3 scallions, white and pale green parts, thinly sliced**

**8 shiitake mushrooms, sliced ¼ inch thick**

**4 ripe plum tomatoes, seeded and diced**

**¼ cup fresh or frozen corn kernels (do not thaw)**

**2 teaspoons chopped cilantro leaves**

**Kosher salt and freshly ground black pepper to taste**

**4 large Honey-Chipotle *Arepas* (page 38)**

A simple sauté of vegetables on a spicy-sweet *arepa* makes a great lunch or simple dinner with a heart-warming soup like my Black Bean Soup with *Hogo* (page 94).

**In a medium-size nonreactive skillet,** heat the oil over medium-high heat. Add the shallots and cook, stirring, until softened, about 3 minutes. Add the garlic, scallions, mushrooms, tomatoes, and corn and cook, stirring, until softened and beginning to brown, 5 to 8 minutes. Turn off the heat, add the cilantro, season with salt and pepper, and mix well. Slice the *arepas* horizontally in half, as you would an English muffin. Place the filling on the bottom halves and set the tops on the filling. Serve immediately.

# Drinks

Pisco Sours

Brazilian Lime Cocktails (*Caipirinha*)

Passionfruit *Batidas*

Mango Mimosas

Latin Eggnog (*Biblia de Pisco*)

Sparkling Fruit Punch (*Salpicón de Frutas*)

Hot Spiced Brandy (*Canelazos*)

# Pisco Sours

*Makes 6 drinks*

**1½ cups *pisco* (Peruvian grape brandy, found at large liquor stores)**

**¼ cup freshly squeezed lime juice (from about 3 limes)**

**2 tablespoons superfine sugar**

**1 large egg white**

**3 cups crushed ice**

**Angostura bitters (optional)**

When I go to Lima, I don't seem to be able to turn down a Pisco Sour whenever one is offered—meaning that I drink several each day! (Fortunately, the drink isn't too strong.) Peruvians are very proud and fond of this delectable concoction and press it on visitors at every opportunity. I just love the delicate lime flavor and frothy texture. This classic, elegant cocktail makes a perfect introduction to a Bistro Latino–style dinner. They look beautiful in frosted martini glasses; simply place the glasses in the freezer just before your guests arrive. Fresh egg whites are generally much safer than yolks, but, as always, buy them from a store with high turnover (never a farmstand) and keep refrigerated until the last moment.

**Put six heavy tumblers** or martini glasses to chill in the freezer. Place the *pisco,* lime juice, sugar, egg white, and ice in a blender or food processor and process until smooth and foamy. Pour into the chilled glasses and sprinkle a few drops of bitters on top if desired. Serve immediately.

## Brazilian Lime Cocktails (*Caipirinha*)

*Makes 2 drinks*

½ cup freshly squeezed lime juice (from about 6 limes), pineapple juice, or strained strawberry puree

2 teaspoons superfine sugar

2 ounces *cachaça* (found at large liquor stores) or vodka

Ice cubes

The *caipirinha* is the national cocktail of Brazil, and it packs a wallop! *Cachaça* is a Brazilian brandy made from sugarcane: It is very sweet, very delicious, and very strong. The citric note of fresh lime makes it the perfect mixer. These are great for a party, especially if you plan to have your guests dance the samba after dinner. You can substitute fresh pineapple juice for the lime juice, or use strained pureed strawberries to make the drink that bartenders at Bistro Latino call a *Caipirango*.

**Place the lime juice,** sugar, and *cachaça* in a cocktail shaker. Add three or four ice cubes and shake well. Strain into short, heavy glasses filled with ice cubes. Serve immediately.

# Passionfruit Batidas

*Makes 3 to 4 drinks*

**1 pound diced fresh ripe or thawed
    frozen fruit, such as passionfruit,
    mango, blackberry, or cantaloupe**

**1 cup cold water**

**Superfine sugar to taste**

**4 ounces *aguardiente* or Greek ouzo
    (both found at large liquor stores)**

**2 sprigs fresh mint leaves**

**Grenadine (optional)**

**Granulated sugar (optional)**

*F*resh fruit juices or *batidas,* also known as *liquados* or *aguas frescas*, are hugely popular throughout South America. Made with everything from bananas and blackberries to melons and mangoes, there are stands devoted to whipping up these refreshing drinks in every town. In Cartagena, on Colombia's Caribbean coast, a whole street is dedicated to colorful *batida* stands, always run by women and decorated with hanging baskets of at least twenty kinds of fresh fruit. Once you decide which fruit suits your mood, you just have to choose between *agua y leche.* Either ice water or cold milk can provide the liquid for a *batida,* depending on whether you're craving a fresh juice or a fruity milk shake.

This cocktail *batida* uses *aguardiente* (an anise-flavored brandy made from sugarcane syrup, it's Colombia's national drink) for some of the liquid, making a very grown-up brunch drink that's perfect with my Shrimp and Lobster Hash Browns (page 125). You can make a batch for the kids by leaving out the *aguardiente* and adding more water or milk. If you like, substitute mango puree or another ripe, sweet fruit for the passionfruit in this recipe. Experiment! There's really no such thing as a bad *batida.*

**In a blender or food processor,** process the fruit and water together until smooth. Sweeten to taste with sugar, add the *aguardiente,* and puree again. Pour into a pitcher and garnish with the mint sprigs. Chill until ready to serve and stir just before serving.

As an additional garnish, dip the glass rim in grenadine and then in granulated sugar, if desired.

# Mango Mimosas

*Makes 4 to 6 drinks*

**8 ounces thawed frozen mango puree
or 1 cup pureed fresh mango pulp
(from about 1 mango)**

**1 bottle chilled Champagne or other
dry sparkling wine**

Here's another marvelous drink for brunch, with a vivid mango taste that wakes up drowsing morning appetites. You can also substitute freshly squeezed orange juice for half of the mango puree.

**Strain the mango puree** through a fine-mesh sieve to remove the fibers. When ready to serve, gently pour the wine into a large bowl. Mix in the mango puree just until combined, being careful not to beat or whisk the mixture. Ladle into cups and serve immediately.

# Latin Eggnog (*Biblia de Pisco*)

Makes 4 to 6 drinks

**8 large eggs**

**½ cup superfine sugar**

**1½ cups *pisco* (found at large liquor stores)**

**½ teaspoon ground cinnamon**

**A** luscious drink that can be described as a sort of Latin eggnog, made with the Peruvian grape brandy called *pisco* instead of rum or brandy. It is always drunk around Christmastime. To minimize the risk of salmonella (because the eggs are not cooked), make sure that you use the very freshest eggs from a store with good turnover (never from a farmstand) and keep them refrigerated until the last moment.

**In a large serving bowl,** whisk the eggs and sugar together until very frothy. Add the *pisco* and whisk together. Chill at least 2 hours until ready to serve. Serve sprinkled with cinnamon and keep any extra refrigerated.

# Sparkling Fruit Punch (*Salpicón de Frutas*)

Makes 4 to 6 servings

**1 cup peeled and diced fresh pineapple**

**1 banana, peeled and cut into**
   **¼-inch dice**

**2 navel oranges, peeled, white pith**
   **cleaned away, and cut into**
   **¼-inch dice**

**½ small papaya, peeled, seeded, and**
   **cut into ¼-inch dice**

**2½ cups chilled cranberry juice**

**1 cup chilled lemon-lime soda**

**Ice cubes**

**Fresh mint sprigs for garnish**

I always serve this at my daughter Amanda's birthday parties, but I've noticed that adults like it too. It has the fruity, festive effect of sangria—without the alcohol.

**Combine all the ingredients,** except the ice and garnish, in a pitcher or punch bowl. Serve over ice, garnished with mint sprigs.

# Hot Spiced Brandy (Canelazos)

*Makes 4 drinks*

1 cup *aguardiente* (Colombian anise–flavored brandy, found at large liquor stores) or Greek ouzo

6 cups water

1 pound *panela* (page 5) or light brown sugar

6 cloves

2 tablespoons ground cinnamon

Coarse sugar, for coating glass rims (optional)

If you like mulled wine or hot cider, *canelazos* will become a wintertime favorite in your house. Even in the summer, nights can be cold in the high mountains around the city of Bogotá. The hostesses in the restaurants there hand you a steaming glass of cinnamon-spiked *canelazos* when you arrive to warm you as you look at the menu—and the spectacular view of the city below. Meant to be drunk in small quantities, it is quite sweet and strong—feel free to use less sugar and more water if desired.

**In a large saucepan,** combine all of the ingredients and heat to a simmer. Simmer until the sugar is dissolved. Serve very hot in small glasses, rimmed with coarse sugar if desired.

# Appetizers

Fresh Salmon Tartare

Tuna Ceviche with Coconut

Ecuadoran Mixed Seafood Ceviche

Miraflores Peruvian Ceviche

Fresh Mushroom Ceviche with Scallions

Swordfish *Escabeche*

Duck Breast *Escabeche*

Shrimp in Cilantro and Garlic Oil
   (*Camarones al Ajillo*)

Latin Crab Cakes

Colombian Sirloin Empanadas

Chicken Empanadas with Garlic-Parsley Crust

Spicy Vegetable Empanadas

Goat Cheese and Basil Tamales

Shrimp and Plantain Tamales

# Fresh Salmon Tartare

**Makes 6 servings**

1 pound very fresh salmon fillets, skin
    removed

2 tablespoons finely minced red onion

2 teaspoons drained capers, chopped

2 teaspoons Dijon mustard

1 tablespoon finely chopped cilantro
    leaves

1 teaspoon kosher salt

½ teaspoon freshly ground black
    pepper

½ lemon, seeded

*E*veryone loves the bright, fresh flavors of this simple dish accented with lemon and capers. You can serve it as a dip for plantain or tortilla chips, or scoop it onto individual plates with a salad of baby greens for an elegant appetizer. Chop the salmon fine with a sharp knife; if you use the food processor, you'll end up with a mushy salmon spread—not what you want. This recipe also adapts well to fresh tuna; try adding 2 teaspoons each of soy sauce and toasted sesame seeds, and substituting minced scallion for the cilantro.

As always when working with raw fish, buy the highest-quality, never-frozen salmon for this dish, from the most reputable fishmonger you know who understands you will be eating this raw. In terms of both flavor and safety, it's worth the extra effort and money.

**With a sharp knife,** chop the salmon very finely. (Do not use the food processor; see above.) Put the salmon in a bowl and add the onion, capers, mustard, cilantro, salt, and pepper. Mix gently, just until combined, and refrigerate at least 1 hour, until ready to serve. Just before serving, squeeze the lemon over the top, mix gently, and season again with salt and pepper. Serve chilled with vegetable chips.

# Tuna Ceviche with Coconut

*Makes 6 servings*

**1 pound best-quality fresh tuna, cut into ¼-inch dice**

**Freshly squeezed juice of 6 limes (about ½ cup)**

**2 teaspoons prepared horseradish, such as Gold's**

**2 teaspoons peeled and finely grated fresh ginger**

**1 cup peeled and diced fresh pineapple**

**1 cup unsweetened coconut milk (page 4)**

**¾ cup cream of coconut (page 4)**

**1 teaspoon chipotle puree (page 3), or more to taste**

To Latin American cooks, there is a clear distinction between the first and second pressings of coconut milk, not unlike the distinctions made in Italy between pressings of olive oil. The first pressing (pure coconut liquid) is thick and oily, the second (which combines the coconut flesh with water) clear and delicate.

In Colombia, this ceviche is made in two stages: First, the fish is combined with lime juice and marinated; then, the second-press coconut milk is added and a second marination takes place. Don't let it "cook" too long; the fish should still be soft. The luscious lime-coconut flavor here is enhanced by Asian seasonings for a very special ceviche. And since some culinary historians believe that the ceviche technique made its way to Latin America from Asia, the flavorings are quite appropriate.

**Place the tuna** in a glass or ceramic bowl. Add the lime juice, mix well, cover tightly, and refrigerate for 15 minutes. Add the remaining ingredients, mix well, and refrigerate another 15 minutes before serving. The tuna should be turning opaque, but still be red in the center and tender to the bite. Serve chilled.

# Ecuadoran Mixed Seafood Ceviche

mixed seafood ceviche

Makes 8 servings

One 8-ounce best-quality fresh tuna
   steak, cut into ½-inch dice

8 ounces best-quality fresh bay or sea
   scallops (if using sea scallops, cut
   them in half)

One 8-ounce best-quality fresh
   swordfish steak, cut into ½-inch dice

10 limes, seeded and quartered

3 lemons, seeded and quartered

1 orange, seeded and quartered

1 ripe Hass avocado, pitted, peeled,
   and cut into ½-inch dice

½ medium-size red onion, finely diced

1 cup coarsely chopped cilantro leaves

1 cup tomato juice

2 tablespoons ketchup

1 teaspoon Tabasco sauce, or more to
   taste

2 tablespoons extra-virgin olive oil

Freshly squeezed juice of 1 lime

Kosher salt and freshly ground black
   pepper to taste

South America has as many ways to make ceviche as it has cooks. Ceviche—marinated raw fish—is a wonderful hot-weather dish, requiring minimal preparation and cleanup and absolutely no time at the stove. Instead of heat, the natural acids in the lime, orange, and tomato juices do the cooking. The spicy, tomato-rich marinade in this version reminds me of a piquant cocktail sauce, and is typical of the ceviches of Quito, Ecuador's capital. I like to serve ceviche in elegant martini glasses, with plantain chips and a sprig of cilantro for garnish.

**Combine the fish** in a large glass or ceramic bowl. Squeeze the limes, lemons, and orange over, mix well, cover tightly, and refrigerate at least 12 hours before serving. Stir the mixture occasionally to ensure even marinating. When "cooked," the fish will be firm and opaque. When ready to serve, strain the fish and discard the marinade. Add the avocado, onion, cilantro, tomato juice, ketchup, Tabasco, olive oil, and lime juice to the fish and mix gently to combine. Season with salt and pepper and serve chilled.

# Miraflores Peruvian Ceviche

Makes 8 servings

2 pounds best-quality fresh striped
   bass or other sea bass fillets,
   skinned and cut into ½ × 1½-inch
   strips
4 ears fresh corn, husked and kernels
   cut off the cob
1 small red onion, quartered and thinly
   sliced
1 small jalapeño pepper (optional),
   seeded and finely minced
Freshly squeezed juice of 12 limes
   (about 1 cup)
1 teaspoon kosher salt
1 tablespoon chopped fresh parsley
   leaves

Miraflores is the leafiest district of Lima, a city packed with *cebicherias* (ceviche stands) and seafood restaurants. In addition to ceviches of clam, conch, shrimp, snapper, mackerel, and countless others, I discovered there a lively concoction called *leche de tigre*—tiger's milk. Limeños are so dedicated to ceviche that they drink the lime juice the ceviche is marinated in, spiked with plenty of sea salt, as a remedy for too many Pisco Sours (page 53) the night before.

In Lima, ceviche is generally served with thick slices of baked sweet potato and corn on the cob, both of which provide a perfect sweet, starchy balance for the citric fish. I had a wonderful one at Punta Sal, a *cebicheria* near Lima's Parque de Amor, the Park of Love—which lives up to its name until long past midnight. Sometimes it seems as if every young couple in Peru is promenading there! But occasionally they take a break from kissing for a ceviche like this one.

**In a large glass** or ceramic bowl, combine the fish with the corn kernels, onion, and jalapeño, if using. Add the lime juice, salt, and parsley and toss to combine. Cover tightly and refrigerate for 30 minutes to 1 hour, until the fish is just beginning to turn opaque but is still moist inside. Stir occasionally to ensure even marination. Serve chilled.

# Fresh Mushroom Ceviche with Scallions

*Makes 4 servings*

**8 ounces shiitake mushrooms, stems removed and caps quartered**

**½ cup fresh or thawed frozen corn kernels**

**½ small red onion, finely diced**

**2 scallions, white and pale green parts, thinly sliced**

**1 teaspoon finely chopped fresh parsley leaves**

**1 teaspoon finely chopped cilantro leaves**

**Freshly squeezed juice of 6 limes (about ½ cup)**

**2 pinches of kosher salt**

**1 medium-size carrot, sliced ¼ inch thick**

**1 tablespoon firmly packed dark brown sugar**

**2 cups cold water**

**Extra-virgin olive oil**

Chefs in the cosmopolitan city of Lima are justifiably proud of the varied cuisine of Peru, generally considered the most sophisticated in South America. At Las Brujas de Cachiche (The Witches of Cachiche, a renowned local community of healers), one of the city's finest and most beautiful restaurants, many of the dishes include only pre-Columbian ingredients and are based on the traditional foods of the Incas. That isn't quite true of this dish—both onions and carrots were introduced to the continent more recently—but this is a wonderfully refreshing appetizer I first had there. It's a great alternative to the usual green salad before dinner.

**Combine the mushrooms,** corn, onion, scallions, parsley, and cilantro in a medium-size glass or ceramic bowl. Add the lime juice and salt, mix well, cover, and refrigerate while you prepare the carrot.

Place the carrot and sugar in a small saucepan and add the water. Cover, bring to a boil, and simmer until the carrot slices are just tender all the way through, 10 to 15 minutes. Drain well and plunge into ice water to stop the cooking. Drain and chill for 10 minutes. Add the carrot to the mushroom mixture, mix well, and serve as soon as possible, drizzled with olive oil.

# Swordfish Escabeche

*Makes 4 servings*

**Two 8-ounce swordfish steaks, ¾ inch thick**

**Kosher salt and freshly ground black pepper to taste**

**2 tablespoons olive oil**

**½ medium-size red onion, thinly sliced**

**1 garlic clove, minced**

**½ large red bell pepper, seeded and sliced into thin rings or strips**

**2 tablespoons chopped pimento-stuffed olives**

**1 tablespoon chopped cilantro leaves**

**1 teaspoon chopped fresh thyme leaves**

**2 tablespoons best-quality red wine vinegar or sherry vinegar**

**Pinch of ground cumin**

**1 tablespoon chopped fresh chives**

*E*scabeche is a very old method of preserving food in vinegar that was created by the Arabs, then adapted by the Spaniards, and now utterly assimilated into Latin American kitchens. This dish is equally at home in all three cuisines, with its tart, spicy, and salty notes. Meaty swordfish is a natural for *escabeche,* since the vinegar in the dish can cause flakier fish to disintegrate. For the best flavor, pay attention to the quality of the vinegar you use—it shouldn't be too harsh.

**Season the swordfish** on both sides with salt and pepper. In a large nonreactive skillet, heat the oil over high heat. Add the fish and quickly brown on both sides. Add the onion, garlic, red pepper, and olives, reduce the heat to medium and cook, stirring, just until the vegetables are softened, 5 to 8 minutes. The fish should be cooked through but not dry. Add the cilantro and thyme, stir, and pour in the vinegar. Sprinkle the cumin over, stir to scrape the bottom of the pan, and turn off the heat. Add salt and pepper to taste. Serve immediately or at room temperature, sprinkled with chives.

# Duck Breast *Escabeche*

Makes 4 servings

- 2 teaspoons olive oil
- 1 medium-size red onion, thinly sliced
- 4 duck breast halves (also called magrets), skinned and cut crosswise into ½-inch-wide strips
- 2 teaspoons minced garlic
- 1½ teaspoons chopped fresh oregano leaves
- 1 bay leaf
- ½ cup full-bodied, dry red wine, such as Cabernet Sauvignon
- 1 cup Chicken Stock (page 32) or canned low-sodium chicken broth
- Kosher salt and freshly ground black pepper to taste
- 2 tablespoons brine-cured black olives, such as Kalamata or Niçoise, pitted and quartered
- 1 red bell pepper, seeded and cut into thin strips
- 1 yellow bell pepper, seeded and cut into thin strips

The balanced combination of intense flavorings in this dish—garlic, oregano, red wine—is the perfect counterpoint to rich duck meat. Boned duck breasts are expensive, but wonderfully easy, quick, and delicious.

**In a large nonreactive skillet,** heat the oil over medium-high heat. Add the onion and cook, stirring, until softened. Raise the heat to high and add the duck to the skillet, a few pieces at a time. Cook just until browned, then stir in the garlic, oregano, and bay leaf. Add the wine to the skillet and cook over high heat until reduced by three quarters to a thick glaze. Add the stock and cook until reduced by about half. The duck should be just cooked through. Season with salt and pepper. Serve immediately or at room temperature, sprinkled with the olives and pepper slivers.

# Shrimp in Cilantro and Garlic Oil (*Camarones al Ajillo*)

*Makes 4 servings*

**2 pounds medium-size shrimp in their shells, heads and tails left on**

**1 cup extra-virgin olive oil**

**3 large garlic cloves, chopped**

**1 cup chopped cilantro leaves**

**3 tablespoons kosher salt**

*T*his classic Spanish dish, equally popular in South America, is both easy to make and fun to eat. Cooking the shrimp in the shells gives them a marvelous flavor, enhanced by the olive oil–cilantro cooking bath. Everyone just dips into the casserole, peels the shrimp with their fingers, and pops them into their mouths. This recipe can easily be doubled or even tripled for a crowd—just make sure to cover your table (and guests) with butcher paper or newspaper to catch the delicious garlic oil. Crusty bread is a must for this dish. To serve as an entree, just cook up a batch of nutty Cartagena Coconut-Pineapple Rice (page 170) and spoon the shrimp and sauce on top. The result is outrageously good.

**Preheat the oven** to 400 degrees. Arrange the shrimp in layers in a medium-size glass baking dish, sprinkling each layer with oil, garlic, cilantro, and salt. Bake, uncovered, until golden and the shrimp are opaque, 10 to 12 minutes. Let cool briefly, until the shrimp are cool enough to handle, and serve immediately.

# Latin Crab Cakes

Makes 4 servings

2 tablespoons olive oil

1 small carrot, finely diced

1 small red onion, finely diced

1 poblano chile, fresh or roasted
   (page 6), seeded and finely diced

½ large red bell pepper, seeded and
   finely diced

1 pound lump or jumbo lump
   crabmeat, picked over for shells and
   cartilage

½ cup Chipotle Mayonnaise (page 30)

¼ cup dry bread crumbs

Homemade crab cakes are always more wonderful than restaurant versions, even the popular ones at Bistro Latino. Make them fresh, with just enough bread crumbs to hold them together, and you'll taste the difference. These light crab cakes come together instantly once the vegetables are diced. Serve with Hot Papaya Salsa (page 16).

In a large cast-iron or nonstick skillet, heat the oil over medium-high heat. Add the carrot, onion, poblano, and red pepper and cook, stirring, just until softened, about 3 minutes. Transfer to a medium-size bowl and let cool at least 15 minutes. Rinse out the skillet and wipe it dry with paper towels.

Add the crabmeat, mayonnaise, and bread crumbs to the vegetables and mix gently. With your hands, roll the mixture into golfball–sized balls and place on a baking sheet. Press each ball down with your palm to make cakes about a half inch thick. Reheat the skillet over high heat, adding more oil if necessary. Working in batches, brown the cakes in the skillet, turning once. Serve immediately.

# Colombian Sirloin Empanadas

*Makes about 12 large empanadas*

**For the filling:**

1 cup peeled boiling potatoes cut into
  ¼-inch dice

1 tablespoon plus 1 teaspoon olive oil

2 cups sirloin steak ¼-inch dice

½ cup finely chopped scallions, white
  and pale green parts

1 cup seeded and diced ripe tomatoes

2 teaspoons ground cumin

**For the dough:**

1 teaspoon roasted garlic (page 6)

2 cups fine-ground cornmeal

¼ teaspoon kosher salt

¼ teaspoon freshly ground black
  pepper

½ tablespoon chopped fresh parsley or
  cilantro

2¼ cups hot Chicken Stock (page 32),
  canned low-sodium chicken broth, or
  water

If there is one food that is truly universal in Latin America, it's the empanada—flaky fried pastries stuffed with meat, fish, and vegetables. Mexican, Colombian, Chilean, Argentine, and scores of others all have their own distinct qualities, with different fillings, doughs, and seasonings. For breakfast, lunch, dinner, and anytime in between, empanadas are wildly popular. The half-moon shape I've chosen for my empanadas is the most common and convenient. Just bite off the end, spoon a little *ají verde* into the opening, and repeat—see how easy it is!

**Place the potatoes** in a small saucepan and cover with cold salted water. Cover and bring to a boil, then boil until just tender, about 5 minutes, and drain. Meanwhile, in a large nonreactive skillet, heat 1 tablespoon of the olive oil over medium-high heat. Add the sirloin and cook, stirring occasionally, until browned, about 5 minutes. Add the scallions and cook for 1 minute. Add the tomatoes and cook for 1 minute. Add the cooked potatoes and cumin and cook, stirring occasionally, for 3 minutes. Transfer to a bowl and set aside to cool.

To make the dough, in a large bowl, mix the garlic with the remaining teaspoon olive oil. Add the cornmeal, salt, pepper, and parsley. Add most of the hot stock and mix just until well combined—the dough should be sticky and elastic. Add more stock only if needed. Refrigerate for 10 minutes to let the dough set. Cover your work surface with plastic wrap and turn out the dough onto it. Cover with another sheet of plastic wrap and roll the dough flat with a rolling pin, using short strokes, until it is about ⅛ inch thick. Without removing the plastic wrap, and using a cup about 4 inches in diameter, cut out rounds of dough.

Peel off the top layer of plastic wrap. Clear out the dough between the rounds and reserve. With a pastry brush, brush the edges of each round with the beaten egg. Place a heaping teaspoon of filling on the lower half of each disk. Working on one empanada at a time, grab the plastic wrap and use it to fold the dough over to create a half-moon shape. Pressing through the plastic wrap, gently seal the empanada with the edge of the cup. Remove from the plastic wrap and set aside on a baking sheet. Repeat with the remaining empanadas, rerolling the scraps of dough until it is all used up.

Heat 2 to 3 inches of oil in a heavy medium-size pot, or heat the oil in a deep fryer. When the oil is hot, about 365 degrees (use a bit of leftover dough to test it; the dough should quickly puff and turn gold), drop four empanadas into it and fry until golden. Remove and drain on a wire rack. Repeat with the remaining empanadas. Serve hot with *ají verde*.

To make, cook, and serve:

**1 large egg, lightly beaten**

**Vegetable oil for frying**

**1 recipe *Ají Verde* (page 10)**

# Chicken Empanadas with Garlic-Parsley Crust

*Makes about 10 large empanadas*

*For the filling:*

**2 tablespoons olive oil**

**1 teaspoon roasted garlic (page 6)**

**1 pound boneless chicken or duck breasts, preferably free range, skinned and cut into ¼-inch dice**

**1 pound cooked yuca (page 8), cut into ¼-inch dice**

**1 teaspoon chopped fresh thyme leaves**

**½ teaspoon sazón Goya (page 6)**

**1 pinch of ground cumin**

**1 teaspoon chopped fresh chives**

*T*his savory but mild empanada is particularly flexible in its flavors—it's good for lunch, as an appetizer, with cocktails, or, made in sufficient quantity, as a great casual dinner served with a big salad like my Arugula Salad with Lentils and Plantains (page 86).

**In a large skillet,** heat the oil over high heat. Add the garlic and stir. Add the chicken, yuca, thyme, sazón, and cumin and cook, stirring occasionally, until the chicken is browned, 5 to 8 minutes. Transfer to a bowl, add the chives, mix well, cover, and refrigerate while you make the dough.

In a large bowl, mix together the garlic and olive oil. Add the cornmeal, salt, pepper, and parsley. Add most of the hot stock and mix just until well combined—the dough should be sticky and elastic. Add more stock only if needed. Refrigerate for 10 minutes to let the dough set. Cover your work surface with plastic wrap and turn out the dough onto it. Cover with another sheet of plastic wrap and roll the dough flat with a rolling pin until it is about ⅛ inch thick. Without removing the plastic wrap, and using a cup about 4 inches in diameter, cut out rounds of dough.

Peel off the top layer of plastic wrap. Clear out the dough between the rounds and reserve. With a pastry brush, brush the edges of each round with the beaten egg. Place a heaping teaspoon of filling on the lower

*For the dough:*

**1 teaspoon roasted garlic (page 6)**

**1 teaspoon olive oil**

**2 cups fine-ground cornmeal**

**½ teaspoon kosher salt**

**¼ teaspoon freshly ground black pepper**

**½ tablespoon chopped fresh parsley or cilantro leaves**

**2¼ cups hot Chicken Stock (page 32), canned low-sodium chicken broth, or water**

*To make, cook, and serve:*

**1 large egg, lightly beaten**

**Vegetable oil for frying**

**1 recipe *Ají* (optional; page 9)**

half of each disk. Working on one empanada at a time, grab the plastic wrap and use it to fold the dough over to create a half-moon shape. Pressing through the plastic wrap, gently seal the empanada with the edge of the cup. Remove from the plastic wrap and set aside on a baking sheet. Repeat with the remaining empanadas, rerolling the scraps of dough until it is all used up.

Heat 2 to 3 inches of oil in a heavy medium-size pot. When the oil is hot, about 365 degrees (use a bit of leftover dough to test it; the dough should quickly puff and turn gold), drop four empanadas into it and fry until pale golden brown. Remove and drain on a wire rack. Repeat with the remaining empanadas. Serve hot with *ají*.

# Spicy Vegetable Empanadas

*Makes about 12 large empanadas*

## For the filling:

2 tablespoons olive oil

1 teaspoon minced shallots

1 cup thinly sliced scallions, white and
   pale green parts

1 cup sliced shiitake mushroom caps

½ cup fresh or frozen green peas

12 ounces cooked yuca (page 8), cut
   into ¼-inch dice

1 teaspoon sazón Goya (page 6)

½ cup *Hogo* (page 11)

2 teaspoons chipotle puree (page 3)

Kosher salt and freshly ground black
   pepper to taste

*I*t truly amazes me how one food—empanadas—can be so popular all over a continent as large and diverse as South America. Everywhere you go, the tempting golden puffs are stacked up, waiting to be quick-fried to your order. As street food, they're even more convenient than hot dogs. But empanadas are equally at home in restaurants and home kitchens. This all-vegetable empanada presents a lightly sweet plantain crust stuffed with a fresh-tasting mushroom-scallion filling touched with hot, smoky chipotle. The key to this dough is using the absolute ripest plantains—soft, limp, and black.

**In a large skillet,** heat the oil over medium-high heat. Add the shallots, scallions, and mushrooms and cook, stirring, until softened, about 5 minutes. Add the peas, yuca, sazón, *hogo,* and chipotle and stir to heat through. Season with salt and pepper and set aside to cool to room temperature.

Preheat the oven to 350 degrees. Place the hot, fried plantains in a large bowl and mash. Add the honey and 6 tablespoons of the bread crumbs. Mix until the dough comes together and is still a bit sticky, adding more bread crumbs only if needed. Refrigerate for 10 minutes to let the dough set. Cover a work surface with

**For the dough:**

**3 very ripe large plantains, peeled (page 5), sliced ¼ inch thick, and freshly fried as for *Patacones* (page 166)**

**2 tablespoons honey**

**6 to 8 tablespoons dry bread crumbs**

plastic wrap and turn out the dough onto it. Cover with another sheet of plastic wrap and roll the dough flat with a rolling pin, using short strokes, until it is about ⅛ inch thick. Without removing the plastic wrap, and using a cup about 4 inches in diameter, cut out rounds of dough.

Peel off the top layer of plastic wrap. Clear out the dough between the rounds and reserve. Place a heaping teaspoon of filling on the lower half of each disk. Working on one empanada at a time, grab the plastic wrap and use it to fold the dough over to create a half-moon shape. Through the plastic wrap, gently seal the empanada with the edge of the cup. Remove from the plastic wrap and set aside on a baking sheet. Repeat with the remaining empanadas, rerolling the scraps of dough until it is all used up. Bake until crisp and hot, 15 to 20 minutes. Serve immediately.

# Goat Cheese and Basil Tamales

Makes 8 to 10 tamales

2 cups fine-ground cornmeal

2 cups boiling water

1 tablespoon kosher salt

2 tablespoons fresh goat cheese

2 tablespoons finely shredded fresh
basil leaves

½ cup chopped sun-dried tomatoes
(oil-packed or reconstituted dried;
optional)

8 to 10 fresh or thawed frozen banana
leaves, or sheets of parchment
paper, about 12 × 15 inches each

8 to 10 thin strips banana leaf or
kitchen string for tying

Corn and cheese is a wonderful combination . . . and so is cheese and basil . . . and so is basil and corn! These delectable morsels—somewhere between a corn muffin and *polenta*—are one of my customers' favorite examples of Bistro Latino cooking, with an irresistible blending of Latin and Mediterranean influences. In Latin America, banana leaves are almost always used for wrapping tamales—they are sturdy, easy to work with, and impart a bit of fresh flavor to everything they wrap. But parchment paper will certainly do the job, as will corn husks. Serve with *Hogo* (page 11) or *Ají* (page 9).

**Place the cornmeal** in a large glass or ceramic bowl and add half of the water. Mix well. Keep adding water ½ cup at a time until the mixture holds together and is faintly sticky to the touch. Mix in the salt, cheese, basil, and tomatoes, if using. Let rest, covered, for 10 minutes.

Wipe a banana leaf clean with a clean, damp kitchen cloth and lay it lengthwise on your work surface, with the grain running from left to right. Mound about ¼ cup of the filling in the center of the leaf. As if wrapping a present, fold the top down over the filling, pressing lightly, then fold the bottom up to cover. Fold the ends into the center and turn the *tamal* over. Again as if wrapping a present, tie the *tamal* securely closed. Repeat with remaining filling and wrappers.

Arrange a steamer in a pot with a tight-fitting lid filled with a couple of inches of water. Bring to a boil (it should not touch the steamer), place the tamales in the steamer, and steam until heated through and firm, 30 to 45 minutes. Serve still wrapped and let your guests carefully cut the tamales open.

## Shrimp and Plantain Tamales

*Makes 8 to 10 tamales*

**3 tablespoons olive oil**

**2 very ripe plantains, peeled (page 5) and cut into 1-inch-thick slices**

**2 ripe plum tomatoes, cut into ¼-inch dice**

**½ medium-size red onion, cut into ¼-inch dice**

**¼ teaspoon sazón Goya (page 6)**

**8 large shrimp, peeled, deveined, and cut into ½-inch-thick slices**

**1 tablespoon finely chopped cilantro leaves**

**8 to 10 fresh or thawed frozen banana leaves, or sheets of parchment paper, about 12 × 15 inches each**

**8 to 10 thin strips banana leaf or kitchen string for tying**

Plantains oven-roasted and mashed are an easy, fresh alternative to cornmeal *masa,* or dough, as a filling for tamales. The combination of shrimp and plantains is a common one on the Caribbean coast of Colombia; both have a natural sweetness.

**Preheat the oven** to 375 degrees. Grease a baking dish with 1 tablespoon of the oil, arrange the plantains in the dish, and bake until very soft, about 10 minutes.

Meanwhile, heat 1 tablespoon of the oil in a small nonreactive skillet over medium-high heat. Add the tomatoes, onion, and sazón and cook, stirring, until softened, 3 to 5 minutes. Set aside to cool. In a large glass or ceramic bowl, mash the plantains until smooth. Toss the shrimp with the cilantro and the remaining tablespoon oil, then add to the plantains. Add the tomato-onion mixture and mix everything together.

Wipe a banana leaf clean with a clean, damp kitchen cloth and lay it lengthwise on your work surface, with the grain running from left to right. Mound about ¼ cup of the filling in the center of the leaf. As if wrapping a present, fold the top down over the filling, pressing lightly, then fold the bottom up to cover. Fold the ends into the center and turn the *tamal* over. Again as if wrapping a present, tie the *tamal* securely closed. Repeat with remaining filling and wrappers.

Arrange a steamer in a pot with a tight-fitting lid filled with a couple of inches of water. Bring to a boil (it should not touch the steamer), then place the tamales in the steamer, and steam until heated through and firm, 30 to 45 minutes. Serve still wrapped and let your guests carefully cut the tamales open.

#  Salads

Warm Shrimp, Cucumber, and Avocado
  Salad

Chorizo, Artichoke, and Three-Bean Salad

Cucumber and Chayote Slaw

Arugula Salad with Lentils and Plantains in
  Roasted Red Onion Vinaigrette

Romaine-Pineapple Salad with Yogurt
  and Black Pepper

Purple Potato and Scallion Salad

Avocado Salad with Mixed Greens

Garbanzo Salad

# Warm Shrimp, Cucumber, and Avocado Salad

Makes 4 to 6 servings

16 large shrimp, peeled and deveined

6 tablespoons olive oil

2 garlic cloves, minced

3 tablespoons chopped cilantro leaves

Kosher salt to taste

2 ripe plum tomatoes, seeded and diced

2 medium-size cucumbers, peeled, seeded, and diced

1 ripe Hass avocado, pitted, peeled, and diced

1 small red onion, minced

2 teaspoons distilled white, white wine, or balsamic vinegar

Freshly ground black pepper to taste

1 pound mixed baby salad greens (mesclun), or a mixture of at least three greens such as red leaf, romaine, or Boston lettuce, endive, radicchio, arugula, frisée, or watercress

Tomatoes, potatoes, chile peppers, and corn are New World ingredients that were enthusiastically adopted by European chefs—after some initial resistance. (Tomatoes and potatoes were used as decorative house plants, not as food, for years after their arrival in Europe.) Avocados, however, are still mostly an American taste. I adore them. Creamy and nutty, the yellow-green flesh of an avocado feels wonderful in your mouth, especially when it is paired with firm, sweet shrimp.

**Preheat the oven** to 400 degrees.

Arrange the shrimp in a small baking dish. Drizzle the oil over them, then sprinkle the garlic, cilantro, and salt on top. Bake, uncovered, until the shrimp are pink and opaque, 10 to 12 minutes.

Meanwhile, in a medium-size glass or ceramic bowl, toss the tomatoes, cucumbers, avocado, onion, and vinegar together. Season with salt and pepper. Divide the mesclun among serving plates. On one side of each plate, spoon the tomato mixture on top of the mesclun.

When the shrimp are cooked, let cool briefly, then spoon onto the other side of each plate, on top of the mesclun. Spoon some of the shrimp cooking oil over each plate, grind pepper on top, and serve immediately.

# Chorizo, Artichoke, and Three-Bean Salad

Makes 8 to 10 servings

2 fresh chorizos (page 3), sliced
¼ inch thick

One 8-ounce can cranberry or pink
beans, drained and briefly rinsed

One 8-ounce can garbanzo beans
(chickpeas), drained and briefly
rinsed

One 8-ounce can black beans, drained
and briefly rinsed

3 scallions, white and pale green parts,
thinly sliced

1 small red onion, finely diced

2 teaspoons minced garlic

2 small jalapeño peppers, seeded and
finely diced

One 6-ounce jar marinated artichoke
hearts, drained and quartered

¼ cup Tomato-Thyme Vinaigrette
(page 28) or another vinaigrette

1 tablespoon chopped cilantro leaves

Kosher salt and freshly ground black
pepper to taste

There's a lot going on in this salad—spicy sausages, delicate artichokes, and fresh garlic, onion, and jalapeños for flavor, plus a zesty tomato-thyme dressing. Why would you stop at just three beans when you can have so much more?

**In a medium-size skillet,** brown the chorizos over medium-high heat (don't worry if the slices fall apart). Drain on paper towels and set aside to cool.

In a large glass or ceramic bowl, combine the beans, scallions, onion, garlic, jalapeños, artichoke hearts, and chorizos. Add the vinaigrette and toss well to coat evenly. Add the cilantro and season with salt and pepper. Refrigerate, covered, at least for a half hour or up to 4 hours to let the flavors blend. Serve chilled or at room temperature.

# Cucumber and Chayote Slaw

Makes 4 to 8 servings

½ cup pineapple juice

1 large cucumber, peeled, seeded, and
   halved lengthwise

1 large chayote, peeled, pitted, and
   halved lengthwise

2 cups peeled and diced fresh
   pineapple or papaya

1 teaspoon chipotle puree (page 3)

1 teaspoon Dijon mustard

2 tablespoons light-flavored olive oil

Kosher salt and freshly ground black
   pepper to taste

Cucumber and chayote share a cool, crunchy quality that is beautifully accented by hot, smoky chipotle. The sweetness of pineapple pulls the dish into balance. Chayotes look somewhat like green-skinned pears with white, crisp flesh, but they belong to the gourd family. Buy the firmest, smoothest ones you can find. This makes a stimulating first course or side dish for simple grilled food.

**In a small nonreactive saucepan,** simmer the pineapple juice over medium heat until reduced to 2 tablespoons. Let cool to room temperature.

Thinly slice the cucumber halves crosswise. Transfer to a large glass or ceramic bowl. Thinly slice the chayote halves crosswise and add to the bowl. Add the pineapple and toss. Whisk the remaining ingredients together with the reduced pineapple juice and pour over the vegetables. Mix well to coat evenly. Serve immediately or refrigerate, covered, up to 4 hours. Mix well before serving and drain off excess liquid if necessary. Serve chilled.

# Arugula Salad with Lentils and Plantains in Roasted Red Onion Vinaigrette

Makes 4 to 8 servings

1½ cups dried brown or green lentils,
    picked over and rinsed

3 cups Chicken Stock (page 32),
    Vegetable Stock (page 34), or
    canned low-sodium broth

2 tablespoons olive oil

¼ cup diced red onion

3 ripe plum tomatoes, seeded and
    coarsely chopped

3 to 4 tablespoons vegetable oil

2 ripe plantains, peeled (page 5) and
    sliced ½ inch thick

4 bunches arugula, well washed and
    tough stems discarded

1 recipe Roasted Red Onion Vinaigrette
    (page 27)

Kosher salt and freshly ground black
    pepper to taste

There are layers of sweet, spicy onion flavor in this whole-meal salad. The roasted onion gives its rich caramelized flavor to the vinaigrette; the diced fresh onion adds crunch and zing to the dish. Both make a great contrast to hearty lentils, which are very common in the Colombian kitchen, and peppery arugula, which is not. I love the bite of it, though. To speed up the cooking process, cook the lentils the night before you plan to serve the dish.

**Combine the lentils** and stock in a medium-size saucepan. Cover and bring to a boil, then reduce the heat and simmer, adding water if necessary, until the lentils are tender, about 35 minutes. Drain and set aside.

Heat the olive oil in a small nonreactive skillet over medium-high heat. Add the onions and tomatoes and cook, stirring, until softened, about 5 minutes. Remove from the skillet and set aside. Wipe out the skillet with paper towels. Add the vegetable oil to the skillet and heat over medium-high heat. When the oil is hot but not smoking, add the plantains and cook over high heat, stirring occasionally, until golden brown, about 5 minutes. Drain on paper towels.

In a large glass or ceramic bowl, combine the lentils, plantains, arugula, and onion-tomato mixture. Pour about ½ cup vinaigrette over and toss thoroughly to coat evenly. Season with salt and pepper, add more vinaigrette if desired, and serve at room temperature.

# Romaine-Pineapple Salad with Yogurt and Black Pepper

*Makes 6 to 8 servings*

**2 heads romaine lettuce, tough outer leaves removed and discarded**

**2 heads Belgian endive**

**2 cups peeled and diced fresh pineapple**

**One 10-ounce container plain yogurt**

**Kosher salt and freshly ground black pepper to taste**

A couldn't-be-simpler salad, with lots of flavor and texture contrast from the bitter endive, sweet pineapple, cool yogurt, and fresh black pepper. If you know anyone who's watching their fat grams (and who isn't?), they'll love you for making this smooth salad.

**With a large knife,** cut the whole heads of romaine crosswise into 2-inch-thick slices, discarding the base. Wash and dry the sliced leaves. Cut the whole endives crosswise into ½-inch-thick slices, discarding the base. In a large glass or ceramic bowl, combine the dry romaine and endive, separating the leaves with your fingers. Add the pineapple and toss. Spoon the yogurt over and toss gently to coat evenly. Season with salt and pepper and serve immediately, or cover and refrigerate up to 4 hours before serving.

# Purple Potato
and Scallion
Salad

Makes 8 to 10 servings

2 pounds small- to medium-size purple
   potatoes (do not peel)

1 tablespoon kosher salt

1 yellow or red bell pepper, seeded
   and cut into 1/4-inch dice

2 medium-size carrots, thinly sliced

1 large red onion, very thinly sliced

6 scallions, white and pale green parts,
   thinly sliced

1/4 cup chopped oil-cured black olives

3 tablespoons coarse-ground mustard,
   such as Pommery

3 tablespoons distilled white or white
   wine vinegar

1 1/2 teaspoons roasted garlic (page 6)

1 tablespoon chopped fresh thyme
   leaves

2 teaspoons chipotle puree (page 3), or
   more to taste

1/4 cup olive oil

Freshly ground black pepper to taste

Hundreds of varieties of potatoes were known and respected by the Incas of Peru, who were so dedicated to the tuber that they invented an early form of freeze-drying to preserve them.

Purple potatoes, recently introduced to this country, are quite starchy, making them an excellent choice for potato salad. They soak up dressing beautifully. The colors of this salad—purple potatoes, red and yellow peppers, orange carrots, green scallions, and black olives—make it extremely festive. If you do not have access to purple potatoes, try Yukon Golds or peeled Idahos.

**Place the potatoes** in a large saucepan, cover with cold water, and add the salt. Cover, bring to a boil, and continue to boil until the potatoes are cooked all the way through, 12 to 15 minutes. Drain and set aside. Meanwhile, combine the yellow pepper, carrots, onion, scallions, and olives in a large glass or ceramic bowl. In a small bowl, whisk together the mustard, vinegar, garlic, thyme, and chipotle puree. Gradually whisk in the oil.

When the potatoes are cool enough to handle, slice or cut into small chunks, or coarsely mash them. Add the potatoes to the vegetables in the bowl and pour on enough dressing to moisten. Toss well to coat evenly, season with salt and pepper, and add more dressing as needed. Serve at room temperature or refrigerate, covered, up to two days.

## Avocado Salad with Mixed Greens

Makes 6 to 8 servings

6 tablespoons extra-virgin olive oil

3 tablespoons red wine vinegar or
  white wine vinegar

Kosher salt and freshly ground black
  pepper to taste

2 large ripe Hass avocados, pitted,
  peeled, and halved lengthwise

6 cups mixed baby salad greens
  (mesclun), or a mixture of at least
  three greens such as red leaf,
  romaine, or Boston lettuce, endive,
  radicchio, arugula, frisée, or
  watercress

Nothing's more soothing than the creamy flesh of a ripe avocado—whether you need to cool down from a hot day or from a hot meal. Use dark, rough-skinned California Hass avocados for the best flavor. This is a perfectly simple recipe that goes well with many entrees, especially my Chicken Breasts Stuffed with Chorizo, Goat Cheese, and Scallions (page 130). It's a great counterpoint to steamy, savory stews like Aromatic Braised Oxtail with Yuca, Potatoes, and *Hogo* (page 112) as well.

**In a small glass or ceramic bowl,** whisk together the oil, vinegar, and salt and pepper. Set aside.

Cut each avocado half in half again, lengthwise. With the tip of the knife, slice each quarter lengthwise into ⅛-inch-thick slices. Whisk the vinaigrette together again. In a large glass or ceramic bowl, toss the greens with the vinaigrette until coated evenly and divide among serving plates. Top with the avocado slices, fanning them out on top of the greens, and grind a little fresh pepper over each plate. Serve immediately.

# Garbanzo Salad

garbanzo salad

*Makes 4 servings*

**Two 8-ounce cans garbanzos (chickpeas), drained and briefly rinsed**

**1 medium-size red onion, cut into ¼-inch dice**

**3 ripe plum tomatoes, seeded and diced**

**3 hard-boiled eggs, peeled and coarsely grated**

**2 teaspoons roasted garlic (page 6)**

**2 tablespoons extra-virgin olive oil**

**2 tablespoons balsamic or white wine vinegar**

**2 tablespoons finely chopped cilantro leaves**

**Kosher salt and freshly ground black pepper to taste**

Garbanzos, or chickpeas (*ceci* in Italian), are a direct link between the traditional cooking of the Mediterranean and that of Latin America. In both realms, humble garbanzos are highly esteemed for their nutty flavor, filling bulk, and excellent nutritional value. I start from scratch with dried chickpeas for this easy salad, but canned are fine—just make sure that you give the salad a few minutes to blend the flavors. It's even better served atop crisp greens.

**In a large glass or ceramic bowl,** combine the garbanzos, onion, tomatoes, and eggs. Whisk the remaining ingredients together. Pour the vinaigrette over the salad, toss well and let stand at room temperature to let the flavors blend, 15 to 20 minutes. Serve immediately or refrigerate, covered, up to 4 hours. Serve at room temperature.

# Soups and Stews

Red Bean–Plantain Soup with Red Wine and Cilantro

Black Bean Soup with *Hogo*

Clota's Plantain Soup

My Father's Potato Soup (*Caldo de Papa de Papi*)

Hearty Barley-Vegetable Soup with Avocado (*Cuchuco*)

My Mother's Bread Soup (*Changua de la Mama*)

Chilled Avocado Soup (*Sopa Fría de Aguacate*)

Fruit Gazpacho

Chilled Melon Soup with Fresh Jalapeño

Clams in Cilantro-Saffron Broth

Ecuadoran Shrimp and Corn Chowder

Red Snapper Soup (*Sancocho de Pescado*)

Honduran Fish Stew with Yuca and Coconut (*Tapado*)

Bogotano Chicken Soup with Capers and Corn (*Ajiaco Santafereño*)

Quick Chicken Stew with Corn (*Estofado de Pollo*)

Chicken in the Pot, Latin Style (*Sancocho de Gallina*)

Chicken, Pork, and Potatoes in Peanut Sauce (*Carapulcra*)

Slow-Cooked Rabbit in Tomato-Coconut Sauce

Aromatic Braised Oxtail with Yuca, Potatoes, and *Hogo*

## Red Bean–Plantain Soup with Red Wine and Cilantro

Makes 6 to 8 servings

¼ cup olive oil

4 ripe plum tomatoes, seeded and
   coarsely chopped

1 medium-size white onion, chopped

2 large garlic cloves, minced

1 ripe plantain, peeled (page 5) and
   sliced ½ inch thick

½ pound dried cranberry, pink, or red
   pinto beans, picked over, rinsed,
   soaked 6 hours or overnight in
   water to cover, and drained

1 meaty smoked ham hock

1 cup dry red wine

10 cups cold water

1 envelope sazón Goya (page 6)

2 cups chopped cilantro leaves

Kosher salt and freshly ground black
   pepper to taste

Dried beans are a staple in most Latin cuisines. They're high in vegetable protein and fiber and low in fat, but more important, they taste great and are extraordinarily versatile. Here they add texture and body to a flavorful soup. This is a perfect example of what I call *Nuevo Mundo* or New World cooking—classic Latin American ingredients and tastes, combined in new ways with new techniques.

**Heat the oil** in a medium-size nonreactive stockpot over medium-high heat. Add the tomatoes, onion, and garlic and cook, stirring, until softened, about 7 minutes. Add the plantain and cook, stirring occasionally, just until softened and golden. Add the beans and ham hock and stir to coat. Add the wine, water, sazón, and cilantro, reserving enough cilantro to sprinkle over the soup as garnish. Simmer, partially uncovered, until the beans are soft, about 1½ hours. Add boiling water as needed to keep the mixture wet.

Remove 2 cups of soup from the pot, puree in a blender or food processor, and stir back into the soup. Season with salt and pepper and serve sprinkled with the reserved cilantro.

# Black Bean Soup with *Hogo*

*Makes 6 to 8 servings*

1 pound dried black beans, picked over, rinsed, soaked 6 hours or overnight in water to cover, and drained

12 cups Chicken Stock (page 32) or canned low-sodium chicken broth

2 meaty smoked ham hocks

2 bay leaves

1 teaspoon ground cumin

1 teaspoon roasted garlic (page 6)

2 carrots, sliced ½ inch thick

1 red onion, thinly sliced

1 small bunch cilantro, roots and stems discarded, leaves coarsely chopped

*Hogo* (page 11)

*Crema agria* (page 4), sour cream, or plain yogurt

In cold weather (very common in high Andean cities like Bogotá and Quito, Ecuador's beautiful capital), there's nothing like a fortifying supper of bean soup. Black beans have excellent texture, but their flavor can be monotonous without strategic seasoning. My favorite solution: the rich, meaty smokiness of ham hocks. Many chefs add a ham hock to the cooking liquid in bean soup, but I don't know of any other recipe where the meat is actually pureed with the soup. The result is smoky, velvety, and delicious.

**Place the beans** in a large pot and add the stock, ham hocks, bay leaves, cumin, and garlic. Bring the mixture to a boil, then reduce the heat and simmer, covered, about 1 hour. Add boiling water as needed to keep the mixture wet. Start tasting the beans after 45 minutes; when they are almost cooked, remove the ham hocks, add the carrots and onion and cook 15 minutes more. When the ham hocks are cool enough to handle, remove the meat from the bones and return it to the soup.

With a hand blender, or working in batches in a blender or food processor, process the soup to a chunky puree. Mix in the cilantro and reheat the soup over low heat if necessary. Serve topped with a spoonful of *hogo* and a spoonful of *crema*.

# Clota's Plantain Soup

Makes 4 servings

2 tablespoons olive oil

8 ounces sirloin steak, trimmed of fat and cut into ½-inch dice

1 small white onion, diced

1 garlic clove, minced

1 large green plantain, peeled (page 5) and coarsely grated

6 cups Chicken Stock (page 32) or canned low-sodium chicken broth

1 small carrot, thinly sliced

Kosher salt and freshly ground black pepper to taste

¼ cup very finely chopped cilantro leaves

One of the best cooks I know is Clota Peña, who has been cooking side-by-side with my Aunt Donna in Bogotá for years. Her delicate but filling *sopa de plátano* is an excellent example of how to achieve vibrant flavor with a few simple ingredients. I have always been impressed by Clota's patience in the kitchen. When I asked her why she bothers to chop the cilantro for this soup into perfect, minuscule shreds, she was surprised that I had to ask. "For the flavor, of course," she answered. And she was completely right.

**In a large, heavy pot,** heat the oil over medium-high heat. Add the steak, onion, and garlic and cook, stirring, until the steak is browned and the onion softened, about 5 minutes. Add the grated plantain and cook, stirring, for 3 minutes. Add the stock, bring to a simmer, and let simmer, partially covered, until the plantain is tender, about 30 minutes. Ten minutes before serving, add the carrot to the pot and season with salt and pepper. Serve sprinkled with the cilantro.

# My Father's Potato Soup (*Caldo de Papa de Papi*)

*Makes 4 to 6 servings*

1 pound beef for boiling, such as shoulder, chuck, or bottom round, cut 1 inch thick (in one piece) and trimmed of fat

2 garlic cloves, very thinly sliced

9 cups cold water

Kosher salt to taste

4 medium-size potatoes, peeled and sliced ⅛ inch thick

6 scallions, white and pale green parts, thinly sliced

1 bunch cilantro, roots and stems discarded, leaves finely chopped

Freshly ground black pepper to taste

*B*oth of my parents are excellent cooks, but it's my father who is really dedicated to the craft. He even makes an art of something as simple as potato soup, by adding raw garlic and beef to the pot. Cooking the meat in one piece, then dicing it and returning it to the soup, gives the soup great flavor and the meat great texture. Don't boil the meat—just barely simmer it.

**Place the beef** and garlic in a large pot. Pour in the water and bring to a simmer over medium heat. Do not boil. Skim off any scum that rises to the top, then simmer until the beef is firm but still pink inside, about 40 minutes. Lift the meat out of the pot and set aside to cool. Taste the liquid and season with salt. When the beef is cool enough to handle, cut it into ½-inch dice. Return the broth to a simmer and add the potatoes, scallions, and beef to the pot. Simmer until the potatoes are cooked through but not falling apart, about 10 minutes. At the last minute before serving, taste for salt again, stir in the cilantro, and season with pepper.

# Hearty Barley-Vegetable Soup with Avocado (*Cuchuco*)

Makes 8 to 10 servings

2 tablespoons olive oil

1 small red onion, diced

1 teaspoon minced garlic

8 ounces cracked or hulled barley (not
   pearl barley), rinsed

3 quarts Chicken Stock (page 32),
   Vegetable Stock (page 34), or
   canned low-sodium broth

1 teaspoon sazón Goya (page 6)

1 cup fresh or frozen green peas

1 cup thinly sliced scallions, white and
   pale green parts

1 cup fresh or frozen corn kernels

Freshly squeezed juice of ½ lemon

Kosher salt and freshly ground black
   pepper to taste

1 ripe Hass avocado, pitted, peeled,
   and thinly sliced

In Colombia, the flavor of this traditional ribsticking soup from the mountains is enriched with pork bones, but I prefer a rich stock. Made with vegetable stock, this becomes a hearty vegetarian soup that works well as an entree with a batch of Honey-Chipotle *Arepas* (page 38).

**In a large, heavy nonreactive pot,** heat the oil over medium-high heat. Add the onion and cook, stirring, until softened, about 5 minutes. Add the garlic and barley and cook, stirring, for 3 minutes. Add the stock and sazón, bring to a simmer, and let simmer gently, uncovered, until the barley is tender, 60 to 80 minutes. Stir in the peas, scallions, corn, and lemon juice and season with salt and pepper. Simmer just until heated through. Serve immediately, topping each serving with sliced avocado.

# My Mother's Bread Soup (*Changua de la Mama*)

Makes 4 to 6 servings

**4 cups cold water**

**2 teaspoons kosher salt**

**3 cups stale bread cubes, preferably from a light, crusty French or Italian loaf**

**2 teaspoons unsalted butter**

**1 cup whole or 2% milk**

**2 large eggs**

**4 ounces lightly salted fresh mozzarella cheese, torn or cut into bite-size pieces**

**2 pinches of sazón Goya (page 6)**

**2 tablespoons finely sliced scallions, white and pale green parts**

**2 tablespoons finely chopped cilantro leaves**

**Freshly ground black pepper to taste**

Of all the Colombian dishes that are reputed to work as a remedy for too much powerful *aguardiente* the night before, *changua* is my favorite. Light, savory, and nourishing, it goes down easily late at night, early in the morning, or any other time you feel like a comforting plate of simple soup. My mother fed me plenty of this in my younger days! It may sound odd at first—a bread-and-milk soup with cheese, scallions, and cilantro—but the taste is immediately familiar and comforting, even though there's nothing quite like *changua* in the American kitchen. Many cooks poach an extra egg for each serving in the simmering soup at the last minute.

**In a large saucepan,** combine the water and salt and bring to a boil. Reduce the heat to a simmer, add the bread, and let simmer until the crusts are soft, about 3 minutes. Stir in the butter and the milk. Break the eggs into the mixture and stir gently with a fork to break them up, then add the mozzarella. Stir in the sazón, and adjust the seasonings with salt and pepper. At the last minute before serving, stir in the scallions and cilantro. Serve hot, sprinkled with black pepper.

## Chilled Avocado Soup (*Sopa Fría de Aguacate*)

Makes 4 to 6 servings

2 ripe Hass avocados, pitted and
   peeled

1 small red onion, coarsely chopped

1 tablespoon roasted garlic (page 6)

4 cups chilled Chicken Stock (page 32)
   or canned low-sodium chicken broth

1 medium-size cucumber, peeled and
   seeded

1 cup shredded fresh spinach leaves

Kosher salt and freshly ground black
   pepper to taste

*T*he creaminess of avocado and the crispness of cucumber effortlessly meld into a cool, green, deliciously simple concoction; eating this is like putting on a fresh white shirt at the end of a steamy summer day. Light in flavor and texture, it's an ideally refreshing appetizer for grilled summer dinners or a perfect lunch when it's too hot to cook.

**Working in batches** if necessary, combine all the ingredients, except the salt and pepper, in a blender or food processor. Process until very smooth and transfer to a serving bowl. Season with salt and pepper. Refrigerate, covered, at least 30 minutes or up to six hours to blend the flavors. Serve cold.

# Fruit Gazpacho

Makes 6 servings

**4 cups pineapple juice**

**2 cups tomato juice**

**3 tablespoons finely chopped cilantro
    leaves**

**1 small red onion, minced**

**1 cup fresh blackberries, left whole**

**1 large ripe peach, peeled, pitted, and
    diced**

**1 cup fresh strawberries, hulled and
    halved**

**Tabasco sauce**

**Kosher salt and freshly ground black
    pepper to taste**

Acid, sweet, sour, cold, fresh—gazpachos have so many wonderful tastes. We call almost any chilled vegetable soup "gazpacho" today, but gazpacho existed in Spain long before New World ingredients like tomatoes and peppers found their way to Europe. In fact, it once had no vegetables in it at all—only bread, almonds, vinegar, and water, which certainly doesn't sound much like soup to us!

My favorite gazpacho is almost as unconventional, combining tomato and onion with juicy-sweet pineapple and bursting-ripe berries, plus cilantro and a dash of hot sauce to pull the flavors together. It couldn't be easier to make—just make sure you serve it very, very cold. For special summer occasions, line bowls with cracked ice and then place smaller bowls of the gazpacho inside.

**Combine all the ingredients** in a glass or ceramic serving bowl, seasoning to taste with Tabasco, salt, and pepper. Mix well. Cover tightly and refrigerate at least two hours or up to six hours to blend the flavors, stirring occasionally. Stir well before serving, adjust the seasonings, and serve very cold.

# Chilled Melon Soup with Fresh Jalapeño

Makes 4 servings

1 very ripe cantaloupe melon, seeded and flesh diced

1 jalapeño pepper, seeded and quartered

⅓ cup aged silver tequila (*añejo*), such as Cuervo 1800

1 cup water

Freshly squeezed juice of 2 limes, or more to taste

1 teaspoon finely chopped cilantro leaves

Sweet cantaloupe and hot jalapeño join in a surprisingly happy marriage in this refreshing no-cook soup. In Latin America, ripe melons and mangoes are often served with chile powder and lime juice to spark the flavors. Tequila also helps liven things up, but you can leave it out if you wish or substitute another liquor such as Peruvian *pisco* or Colombian *aguardiente*.

**Working in two batches** if necessary, combine all the ingredients in a blender or food processor and process until smooth. Transfer to a glass or ceramic serving bowl and refrigerate, covered, at least two hours or up to six hours to blend the flavors. Serve very cold.

# Clams in Cilantro-Saffron Broth

clams in cilantro-saffron broth

*Makes 4 servings*

**4 pounds littleneck clams**

**1½ cups dry, light white wine such as Pinot Grigio**

**¼ cup chopped shallots**

**2 pinches of saffron threads**

**2 tablespoons roasted garlic (page 6)**

**3 cups Fish Stock (page 33) or bottled clam juice, at room temperature**

**1½ cups seeded and diced ripe tomatoes**

**½ cup thinly sliced scallions, white and pale green parts**

**3 tablespoons chopped cilantro leaves**

*I*n hundreds of different shapes and species, and in thousands upon thousands of recipes, clams are harvested and eaten all over the world. The sweet *almejas* of South America's Pacific waters respond beautifully to a quick bubbling in wine and fish stock, creating a dish reminiscent of Italy's many *zuppe di vongole*. With the sweetness of saffron and a green note of cilantro, this simple dish is complete. A pot with a glass lid is particularly handy here, so you can gauge the progress of the clams without lifting the lid.

**Clean the clams:** Put them in the sink and cover them with cold water. Let them sit for 5 minutes, then drain and rinse out the sand that remains. Cover with fresh water, then swish the clams around vigorously in the water, rubbing them against each other to loosen sand and grit. Drain and repeat, if necessary, until no sand remains. Discard any open clams or clams with broken shells.

Place the clams in a large, heavy nonreactive pot with a lid (preferably a glass one) and add the wine, shallots, saffron, and garlic. Cover and bring to a simmer. Cook until the wine is reduced to a syrup. Add the stock, cover, and bring to a simmer. As soon as all the clams have opened (discard any that do not open) and the mixture is heated through, sprinkle the clams with the tomatoes, scallions, and cilantro and serve immediately.

# Ecuadoran Shrimp and Corn Chowder

Makes 4 to 6 servings

¼ cup (½ stick) unsalted butter

2 shallots, minced

6 cups whole milk

½ cup dry, light white wine such as
  Pinot Grigio

Freshly cut kernels from 3 ears corn or
  1½ cups frozen kernels

2 large baking potatoes, peeled and
  cut into ½-inch dice

1 pound medium-size shrimp, peeled
  and deveined

Kosher salt and freshly ground black
  pepper to taste

2 ripe plum tomatoes, seeded and
  finely diced

Chopped cilantro leaves

*S*eafood chowders, or *chupes,* are hugely popular in Ecuador and Peru. The people there would be very surprised to hear that in the States, New Englanders consider chowder their own private property! This is easy, luxuriously rich, yet very light, with a wonderful silky texture. The delicate ocean flavor of shrimp is the perfect counterpoint for sweet corn.

**In a large nonreactive pot,** melt the butter over medium heat. Add the shallots and cook, stirring, until softened, about 3 minutes. Add the milk, wine, and corn and bring to a simmer. Do not boil. Add the potatoes and simmer until almost tender, 12 to 15 minutes. Add the shrimp and salt and pepper to taste and simmer just until opaque, 3 to 5 minutes. Serve hot, garnishing each bowl with a handful of chopped tomatoes and a sprinkle of cilantro.

# Red Snapper Soup (*Sancocho de Pescado*)

red snapper soup

Makes 6 to 8 servings

1 tablespoon olive oil

1 pound fish bones, from snapper, striped bass, or other whitefish (available at your local fish store)

1 medium-size onion, coarsely chopped

4 ripe plum tomatoes, seeded and coarsely chopped

1 cup coarsely chopped cilantro leaves

2 large garlic cloves, minced

2 teaspoons chipotle puree (page 3), or more to taste

1 bay leaf

1 cup dry white wine

8 cups water

2 teaspoons kosher salt, or more to taste

¼ cup peanut or vegetable oil

2 ripe plantains, peeled (page 5) and sliced on the diagonal ¼ inch thick

Freshly ground black pepper to taste

1 cup corn kernels, fresh or thawed frozen

1 large ripe tomato or 2 ripe plum tomatoes, seeded and diced

¼ cup finely chopped scallions, white and pale green parts

This simple fish soup is very close to the spirit and flavor of a classic Mediterranean *soupe de poissons,* with my addition of flavor-rich New World ingredients like cilantro, chipotle, and corn. The deep flavor of the soup is lightened at the table with garnishes of tomato, corn, and scallions. *Patacones* (page 166) are crisp slices of fried plantain that soak up the delicious broth and also make the dish more substantial; in Colombia, they are served alongside all kinds of dishes.

**Heat the oil** in a large, heavy nonreactive pot over medium-high heat. Add the fish bones and cook, stirring, about 3 minutes. Add the onion, plum tomatoes, half of the cilantro, the garlic, chipotle, and bay leaf and cook, stirring, until softened, 5 to 8 minutes. Add the wine and cook over medium heat for about 10 minutes, stirring occasionally, until the liquid is reduced to a syrup. Add the water and salt and simmer, uncovered, until flavorful, 45 minutes to 1 hour.

Meanwhile, make the *patacones:* Heat the peanut oil in a large skillet over high heat until it is hot but not smoking. Add the plantain slices and cook until golden brown on both sides, about 5 minutes. Drain on paper towels. Strain the soup through a fine-mesh strainer into another pot or serving bowls, discarding the fish bones and vegetables. Add the remaining cilantro, taste for salt and pepper, and serve with the *patacones* on top. Pass the corn, diced tomato, and chopped scallions at the table.

# Honduran Fish Stew with Yuca and Coconut (*Tapado*)

*Makes 4 servings*

**8 littleneck clams**

**8 mussels, preferably Prince Edward Island**

**2 cups *Hogo* (page 11)**

**4 cups water**

**1½ cups unsweetened coconut milk (page 4)**

**Kosher salt and freshly ground black pepper to taste**

**4 medium-size potatoes, peeled and sliced ⅛ inch thick**

**1 green plantain, peeled (page 5) and sliced ⅛ inch thick**

**8 ounces cooked yuca (page 8), sliced ⅛ inch thick**

**12 ounces cod fillets, cut into 1-inch pieces**

**8 large shrimp, peeled and deveined**

**2 tablespoons chopped fresh chives**

Fish stews in coconut milk are typical of "Caribbean rim" cooking, and no wonder: It's an unbeatable combination. This special-occasion Honduran dish combines four kinds of seafood with plantain and yuca in a luscious bath of coconut.

**Clean the clams:** Put them in the sink and cover them with cold water. Let them sit for 5 minutes, then drain and rinse out the sand that remains. Cover with fresh water, then swish the clams around vigorously in the water, rubbing them against each other to loosen sand and grit. Drain and repeat, if necessary, until no sand remains. Discard any open clams or clams with broken shells.

Clean the mussels by following the directions for clams, then pull the beard from the side of each mussel with your fingers, or use your fingers and a paring knife for a better grip.

In a large, heavy pot, combine the *hogo,* water, and cream of coconut and bring to a simmer. Season with salt and pepper. Add the potatoes and plantain and simmer until almost tender, 8 to 10 minutes. Add the cooked yuca and clams and simmer 3 minutes more. Add the cod, mussels, and shrimp and simmer just until cooked through, 5 to 7 minutes more. Discard any clams or mussels that do not open. Taste for salt and pepper and serve immediately, sprinkling each plate with chives.

# Bogotano Chicken Soup with Capers and Corn (*Ajiaco Santafereño*)

Makes 6 servings

3 tablespoons olive oil

One 3½- to 4-pound chicken, preferably free range, cut up into serving pieces

1 large white onion, chopped

1 teaspoon minced garlic

2 quarts Chicken Stock (page 32), canned low-sodium chicken broth, or water

1 bunch cilantro, roots and stems discarded, leaves finely chopped

1½ teaspoons dried *guascas*

**A**jiaco is a distinctively Colombian creation and the local pride of the country's capital, Bogotá. (The city's full name is Santa Fe de Bogotá, hence, *Santafereño*.) Essentially a simple chicken soup enriched with potato and corn, then sparked with cilantro and capers, *ajiaco* is both everyday fare and a special occasion soup—my family never seems to get tired of it! *Ajiaco* is a very ancient indigenous dish, but the Spanish population contributed the piquant cream-and-caper garnish, creating the interplay of flavors and textures that makes the soup so haunting. Creamy and sharp, with delicate chicken flavor, *ajiaco* reminds me of *avgolemono*, the classic Greek chicken soup with egg and lemon.

One thing that makes Colombian *ajiaco* so distinctive is the incomparable flavor of *guascas*, an herb that in its dried form smells something like tea leaves. A little bit of dried oregano (not the Mexican kind, which is too strong) can be substituted, although the effect will not be identical.

**In a large, heavy pot,** heat the oil over medium-high heat. Add the chicken pieces and cook just until golden on all sides. Add the onion and garlic and cook, stirring,

**2 large baking potatoes, peeled and very thinly sliced**

**6 new potatoes, halved, or 12 *papas criollas* (page 5), drained**

**12 ounces cooked yuca (optional; page 8), cut into ½-inch dice**

**3 ears fresh corn, husked and cut into 1-inch lengths**

**Kosher salt and freshly ground black pepper to taste**

**2 tablespoons drained capers**

**¼ cup *crema agria* (page 4), crème fraîche, or sour cream**

**1 ripe Hass avocado, pitted, peeled, and thinly sliced**

until softened, about 3 minutes. Add the stock, half of the cilantro, the *guascas* (crumbling it between your fingers), and the baking potatoes. Bring to a simmer, cover, and let simmer gently until the potatoes are falling apart in the soup, about 25 minutes.

Add the new potatoes, if using, and continue cooking until the chicken is tender and the new potatoes are cooked through, about 15 minutes more. When the chicken is cooked, remove it from the pot and set aside. When cool enough to handle, separate the meat from the skin and bones. With your hands, shred into bite-size pieces. Add the chicken meat, *papas criollas,* if using, yuca, if using, and corn to the pot and simmer until heated through. Season with salt and pepper. Serve in shallow bowls, sprinkled with the remaining cilantro, passing the capers, cream, and avocado at the table. The corn pieces should be removed from the soup bowl and set aside to cool, then eaten with the hands.

# Quick Chicken Stew with Corn (*Estofado de Pollo*)

*Makes 2 servings*

**12 ounces skinless, boneless chicken breast, preferably free range, cut crosswise into ½-inch-thick strips**

**Kosher salt and freshly ground black pepper to taste**

**3 tablespoons olive oil**

**1 teaspoon minced garlic**

**1 large ripe tomato, diced**

**8 shiitake or large cremini mushrooms, trimmed and quartered**

**4 medium-size boiling potatoes, quartered lengthwise**

**12 ounces cooked yuca (page 8), cut into ½-inch dice, or additional potatoes**

**3 cups Chicken Stock (page 32) or canned low-sodium chicken broth**

**1 large bay leaf**

**2 ears fresh corn, husked and sliced 1 inch thick**

**2 tablespoons chopped cilantro leaves**

This is delicious proof that a stew doesn't have to take hours on the stove to develop flavor. This is an ideal week-night supper, quickly made with simple ingredients that are often on hand.

**Season the chicken strips** with salt and pepper. In a large, heavy nonreactive pot with a lid, heat the oil over high heat. Add the garlic and stir, then add the chicken strips and cook, stirring occasionally, just until golden brown on all sides, about 3 minutes. Add the tomato, mushrooms, potatoes, and yuca and stir. When the mixture is dry and heated through, add the stock, bay leaf, and corn. Cover, bring to a simmer, and let simmer for 15 minutes. Uncover, season with salt and pepper, and cook until the mixture has the consistency of a stew, about 10 minutes more. Just before serving, stir in the cilantro.

# Chicken in the Pot, Latin Style (*Sancocho de Gallina*)

*Makes 6 to 8 servings*

**One 3½-pound chicken, preferably free range, cut up into serving pieces**

**1 medium-size onion, halved**

**1 medium-size carrot, quartered**

**2 celery stalks, leaves discarded, quartered**

**1 bunch cilantro, roots discarded and washed**

**2 teaspoons kosher salt**

**1 ripe plantain, peeled (page 5) and cut into 1-inch pieces**

**8 ounces thawed frozen yuca, cut into ½-inch dice**

**½ cup coarsely chopped cilantro leaves**

**1 envelope sazón Goya (page 6)**

**12 drained *papas criollas* (page 5) or boiled new potatoes**

**Freshly ground black pepper to taste**

Like *pot-au-feu*, the elemental French farmhouse dinner of boiled meat and vegetables, *sancocho* is an infinitely adaptable dish. *Sancocho* looks a little different in each of the many Latin and Caribbean countries that make it. All agree that it starts as a richly flavored soup of fish or chicken, but each land adds the vegetables it has on hand: calabaza, yams, yuca, potatoes . . . the list goes on and on. This version is very much like the ones I've had in Cartagena, the beautiful capital of coastal Colombia.

**Put the chicken,** onion, carrot, celery, and cilantro in a large, heavy pot and cover with at least 3 quarts water. Add the salt, bring to a boil, reduce the heat to a simmer and cook, uncovered, 45 minutes, stirring occasionally and skimming as necessary to remove scum from the top. Remove the chicken pieces from the pot with a slotted spoon and set aside to cool. When cool enough to handle, remove the chicken meat from the bones. Discard the bones and skin. Remove the vegetables and cilantro from the stock with a slotted spoon and discard.

Add the plantain, yuca, half of the chopped cilantro, and sazón to the stock, return to a simmer, and let simmer until the plantain and yuca are tender, about 30 minutes. Add the remaining ¼ cup cilantro, the *papas criollas* and chicken meat and heat through. Season with salt and pepper and serve hot.

## Chicken, Pork, and Potatoes in Spicy Peanut Sauce (*Carapulcra*)

*Makes 4 to 6 servings*

2 tablespoons olive oil

1 pound pork loin or shoulder, trimmed of fat and cut into ½-inch dice

2 garlic cloves, finely minced

1 pound boneless, skinless chicken breasts or thighs, preferably free range, cut into ½-inch dice

8 to 10 medium-size boiling potatoes, peeled and cut into ½-inch dice

10 cups Chicken Stock (page 32) or canned low-sodium chicken broth

6 tablespoons finely chopped cilantro leaves

2 bay leaves

1 tablespoon chipotle puree (page 3), or more to taste

6 tablespoons peanut butter, preferably organic

Kosher salt and freshly ground black pepper to taste

This classic Peruvian stew is traditionally made with *chuño,* potatoes naturally freeze-dried by the extremely cold, dry air of the Andean highlands. Its savory peanut sauce puts the dish in the family of the *pipián,* dishes made with peanuts or pumpkinseeds. *Pipiáns* are found from Chile to Mexico in many different forms, from peanut–potato tamales in Colombia to Mexican shrimp in pumpkinseed-cilantro salsa. Hot chile and peanuts have a marvelous flavor affinity, very common in Africa and Latin America alike.

**In a large, heavy pot,** heat the oil over medium-high heat. Add the pork and cook, stirring, until browned, about 5 minutes. Add the garlic, chicken, and potatoes and cook, stirring occasionally, until lightly browned, about 8 minutes more. Add the stock, half of the cilantro, the bay leaves, chipotle, and peanut butter. Bring to a simmer, season with salt and pepper, and let simmer gently until it has a stewlike consistency, 30 to 35 minutes. Serve sprinkled with the remaining cilantro.

## Slow-Cooked Rabbit in Tomato-Coconut Sauce

Makes 4 servings

**3 tablespoons apple cider vinegar or white wine vinegar**

**Freshly ground black pepper**

**1 teaspoon ground cumin**

**¼ teaspoon cayenne pepper**

**One 3-pound rabbit, cut up into serving pieces**

**2 tablespoons vegetable oil**

**5 garlic cloves, minced**

**1 medium-size onion, chopped**

**6 to 8 cups Chicken Stock (page 32) or canned low-sodium chicken broth**

**1 tablespoon tomato paste**

**½ cup unsweetened coconut milk (page 4)**

**2 ripe plum tomatoes, peeled, seeded, and chopped**

**Chopped cilantro leaves**

*I*n traditional French bistro cooking as well as in the mountainous Andean regions of South America, rabbit is a popular meat for the stew pot. Since farmed rabbit can be mild in flavor, a brief marination in spices and vinegar followed by slow simmering in a brew that includes tenderizing tomato essence is the key to soft, tasty meat. At the market, be sure to buy unsweetened coconut milk rather than the sweet, thick coconut cream you would use for piña coladas or desserts.

**In a large glass or ceramic dish,** combine the vinegar, 12 grinds of the pepper mill, the cumin, and cayenne. Add the rabbit pieces and mix to coat. Cover and marinate at room temperature for 20 to 30 minutes. Do not overmarinate. Remove the rabbit pieces from the marinade and blot dry on paper towels.

Preheat the oven to 350 degrees. In a large, heavy nonreactive pot that can go in the oven later, heat the oil over medium-high heat. In two batches, brown the rabbit pieces on all sides. Return all the meat to the pot, add the garlic and onion, and cook, stirring, for 3 minutes. Add enough stock to cover the meat and stir, scraping up the browned bits from the bottom of the pan. Heat to a simmer and add the tomato paste, coconut milk, and tomatoes. Cover and bake, stirring every half hour, until the meat is very tender, about 1½ hours. Serve sprinkled with cilantro.

# Aromatic Braised Oxtail with Yuca, Potatoes, and Hogo

Like the classic French beef-and-wine stews served in bistros from Paris to Provence, this makes a wonderfully satisfying meal that only improves with a couple of days in the refrigerator. The yuca and *papas criollas* provide a starchy note, so all you'll need is good bread, a ripe Avocado Salad with Mixed Greens (page 89) alongside, and a bottle of Pinot Noir for toasting the cook.

Makes 4 servings

**8 pounds oxtail, trimmed of fat and cut into 2-inch chunks**

**Kosher salt and freshly ground black pepper to taste**

**¼ cup vegetable oil**

**4 cups dry but fruity red wine, preferably a Chilean Merlot or Pinot Noir such as Los Vascos**

**6 quarts Chicken Stock (page 32) or canned low-sodium chicken broth**

**2 bay leaves**

**2 pounds thawed frozen yuca, cut into 2-inch chunks**

**1 pound drained *papas criollas* (page 5) or raw whole new potatoes**

**2 cups chopped cilantro leaves**

**1 cup *Hogo* (page 11)**

**Season the oxtail** with plenty of salt and pepper. In a large, heavy pot, heat the vegetable oil over high heat. Working in batches to avoid crowding the pot, brown the oxtail on all sides. When all the meat is browned, return it to the pot and add the wine. Cook, uncovered, over medium heat, stirring with a wooden spoon to scrape up the browned bits from the bottom of the pot, until the liquid is reduced and syrupy, about 20 minutes. Add the stock and the bay leaves. Bring to a simmer and cook, uncovered, for 1 hour. Add the yuca and raw new potatoes, if using, and cook until the meat, yuca, and potatoes are tender, about 45 minutes more. When the stew is cooked, add the *papas criollas,* if using, and half of the cilantro. Season with salt and pepper and cook another 5 to 7 minutes to heat through. Serve with a generous sprinkling of the remaining cilantro and a spoonful of *hogo* on top.

## Main Dishes

Summer Vegetable Tart

Venezuelan Eggplant with Green Beans

Pan-Roasted Tuna Steaks with Crisp Yuca Crust

Caramelized Salmon Fillets with Oyster
Mushrooms and Wilted Spinach

Salmon with Saffron (*Salmón ala Safran*)

Pan-Roasted Red Snapper with Garbanzos and
Greens

Fish Baked in Fresh Tangerine Juice and Parsley

Sea Bass and Saffron Risotto

Baked Cod with *Tomaticán*

Martha's Black Bean and Lobster Risotto

Shrimp and Lobster Hash Browns

New World *Paella* (*Paella Nuevo Mundo*)

Shrimp with Coconut Sauce (*Camarones al Coco*)

Rice Simmered with Chicken and Chorizo
(*Arroz con Pollo*)

Chicken Breasts Stuffed with Chorizo, Goat
Cheese, and Scallions

Peruvian Roast Chicken with Purple Potatoes

Roast Chicken with Jalapeños and Yuca
(*Ají de Pollo*)

Roast Turkey with Chorizo-Apple-Cornbread
Stuffing

Chilean Stir-Fried Pork (*Chancho a la Chileña*)

Colombian Rice with Pork Loin, Potatoes, and
Herbs (*Arroz Atollado*)

Tía Donna's Colombian Tamales

Colombian Pot Roast (*Sobrebarriga Bogotano*)

Peruvian Stir-Fried Beef with Onions
(*Lomo Saltado*)

# Summer Vegetable Tart

Makes 4 servings

3 tablespoons unsalted butter

16 shiitake mushrooms, stems removed and caps quartered

4 teaspoons minced shallots

1 cup fresh or frozen green peas

8 to 10 ounces fresh spinach, well washed, and tough stems removed

Kosher salt and freshly ground black pepper to taste

4 teaspoons olive oil

4 red bell peppers, roasted (page 6), peeled, seeded, and cut into strips

4 yellow bell peppers, roasted (page 6), peeled, seeded, and cut into strips

4 large Cheese *Arepas* (optional; page 37)

The bright layers of this vegetable dish make it look impressive, but it's really very easy to put together. There's no crust involved—just creamy white corn cakes (*arepas*, pages 37–40) topped with a round of red and yellow peppers, spinach, and mushrooms bound with their own fresh juices and a bit of butter. Note that you'll need four 8-ounce ramekins to assemble the tarts. Serve with Garbanzo Salad (page 90).

**Preheat the oven** to 350 degrees.

In a large skillet, melt the butter over medium heat. Add the mushrooms and shallots and cook, stirring, until softened, 3 to 5 minutes. Add the peas and spinach and cook just until the spinach is wilted. Drain off any excess liquid. Season with salt and pepper and set aside to cool.

Use the oil to grease four 8-ounce ramekins. Line the bottom of each with a red pepper, then a yellow one. Divide the spinach mixture among the ramekins, pressing down gently to compress. Drain off any excess liquid. Place the ramekins in a roasting pan, then add hot water to the pan until it comes halfway up the sides of the ramekins. Bake until heated through and firm, 10 to 12 minutes. If using *arepas*, arrange them on serving plates. Gently unmold each vegetable tart on top of an *arepa* or onto a plate. Serve immediately or at room temperature.

# Venezuelan Eggplant with Green Beans

Makes 6 servings

3 large eggplants, halved lengthwise

6 tablespoons olive oil

3 garlic cloves, chopped

1 tablespoon unsalted butter

3 cups shiitake mushrooms, stems removed and caps sliced ¼ inch thick

1 cup green beans, blanched until crisp-tender and cut into 1-inch lengths, or thawed frozen green beans

1½ teaspoons minced shallots

1 teaspoon minced garlic

3 ripe plum tomatoes, diced

Kosher salt and freshly ground black pepper to taste

1 tablespoon chopped cilantro leaves

1 tablespoon chopped fresh parsley leaves

**A**lthough Latin Americans do love meat, there is a long tradition of vegetarian dishes, many dating from long before beef and pork were introduced to the continent in the sixteenth century. Eggplants are native to the Andes, but this particular dish may have been developed by Arab immigrants—it's very similar to Middle Eastern recipes for eggplant. It makes a highly satisfying entree, especially with a rice dish like Roasted Corn and Garlic Rice (page 169) alongside.

**On a baking sheet,** combine the eggplant halves, olive oil, and chopped garlic. Toss to coat the eggplant on all sides and let marinate at room temperature for 30 minutes.

Preheat the oven to 325 degrees. Bake the eggplant for 30 minutes, then set aside to cool. When cool enough to handle, scoop out the flesh, leaving about a ¼-inch-thick shell. Transfer the flesh to a large glass or ceramic bowl and arrange the shells on the baking sheet. Mash the eggplant flesh with a fork.

In a large nonreactive skillet, melt the butter over medium-high heat. Add the mushrooms, green beans, shallots, garlic, tomatoes, and salt and pepper to taste and cook, stirring, until softened, 5 to 8 minutes. Transfer to the bowl with the eggplant and mix to combine. Season with salt and pepper. Preheat the oven to 350 degrees. Divide the stuffing among the eggplant shells and bake until heated through and soft, 15 to 20 minutes. Serve sprinkled with cilantro and parsley.

# Pan-Roasted Tuna Steaks with Crisp Yuca Crust

The crunch of this crust is quite spectacular. I love the speed and simplicity of cooking fish fillets and steaks, but without a little texture added they can be unsatisfying. This method takes care of that! The technique works for many kinds of fish (and chips), but tuna steak and yuca is my favorite combination. Terra Chips are widely available in supermarkets; they make both yuca and taro varieties. Almost any kind of thick-cut vegetable chip will work, as long as it is not too oily and salty. Serve this with Cumin Fries (page 160).

**Makes 4 servings**

**3 cups yuca, taro, malanga, or plantain chips**

**Four 6- to 8-ounce tuna steaks, about ¾ inch thick**

**Kosher salt and freshly ground black pepper to taste**

**2 tablespoons olive oil**

**Lemon or lime wedges**

**In a food processor,** pulse the chips into coarse crumbs; do not pulverize to a powder. Spread on a plate. Season the tuna steaks with salt and pepper.

Heat the oil in a large skillet over medium-high heat. Place a tuna steak on the yuca crumbs and press gently to coat the bottom. Turn and repeat. Do not coat the sides of the tuna; just the tops and bottoms. Place in the hot skillet and reduce the heat to medium. Repeat with the remaining tuna. Cook slowly (to prevent the crust from burning) until the crust is golden brown and firm, then carefully turn and cook the other side, 3 to 4 minutes per side. The tuna should be cooked through but not dry; you can check the progress by watching the sides of the steaks. Serve immediately with lemon wedges.

# Caramelized Salmon Fillets with Oyster Mushrooms and Wilted Spinach

*Makes 4 servings*

**2 tablespoons unsalted butter**

**2 shallots, chopped**

**8 ounces oyster mushrooms, torn into quarters, or cremini mushrooms, sliced ¼ inch thick**

**10 ounces fresh spinach, well washed and tough stems removed**

**¼ cup soy sauce mixed with ¼ cup water**

**¼ cup firmly packed *panela* (page 5) or dark brown sugar mixed with ¼ cup water**

**Four 6- to 8-ounce salmon fillets, about ¾ inch thick**

**Chopped cilantro leaves**

*I* (and my customers) love salmon, and when I came up with the idea of giving it a salty-sweet glaze and serving it on fresh, peppery greens, everyone was delighted. I use *panela,* Latin crystallized cane syrup, to caramelize the fish, but brown sugar works just as well when dissolved in water. This is an easy and elegant "company" dish with layers of contrasting flavor. The secret is to simmer the salmon in the caramel instead of browning it as you normally would in a skillet. Serve with Yuca Hash Browns (page 165).

**Melt the butter** in a large nonstick skillet over medium heat. Add the shallots and cook, stirring, until softened, about 3 minutes. Add the mushrooms and cook, stirring, until softened and lightly browned. Add the spinach and cook briefly, just until wilted and softened. Transfer to serving plates.

Rinse out the skillet, wipe it dry with paper towels, and heat it over high heat. When drops of water sizzle on the surface, add the soy mixture and the sugar mixture. Simmer for 1 minute to dissolve the sugar, then arrange the salmon fillets in the pan and reduce the heat to medium. Cook at a simmer (you should see the liquid bubbling rapidly around the fillets), adding more water 2 tablespoons at a time as the mixture cooks dry. When the salmon has firmed up a bit and the underside is glazed, about 3 minutes, turn with tongs and cook 2 to 3 minutes more. Do not overcook—the salmon should remain quite soft. Place the salmon fillets on top of the spinach on the serving plates and serve immediately, sprinkled with cilantro.

# Salmon with Saffron (*Salmón a la Safran*)

## Makes 6 servings

1 teaspoon unsalted butter

Six 6- to 8-ounce salmon fillets, with skin on

Kosher salt and freshly ground black pepper to taste

2 cups Chardonnay or another rich, flavorful white wine

1 teaspoon saffron threads

3 bay leaves

2 teaspoons chopped fresh thyme leaves

2 tablespoons roasted garlic (page 6)

3 ripe plum tomatoes, seeded and diced

1 tablespoon chopped cilantro leaves

1 tablespoon chopped fresh parsley leaves

I love the golden color saffron gives to any dish in which it is cooked. The flavor is not strong, but the aroma adds a wonderful element to this simple bake of salmon, tomatoes, thyme, garlic, and wine. Serve with Colombian Potatoes with Salt and Scallions (page 161).

**Preheat the oven** to 400 degrees. Use the butter to grease a nonreactive baking dish large enough to hold the salmon in a single layer. Arrange the fillets in the pan and season with salt and pepper. Pour the wine around the salmon, just to the tops of the fillets (do not submerge). Place a pinch of saffron on each fillet. Crumble the bay leaves with your fingers and place a pinch on each fillet. Place a pinch of thyme on each fillet. Sprinkle the garlic over the dish, then the tomatoes. Bake, uncovered, just until barely cooked through, 10 to 20 minutes, depending on the thickness of the fillets. Serve sprinkled with the cilantro and parsley.

# Pan-Roasted Red Snapper with Garbanzos and Greens

Although Latin America has hundreds of indigenous bean varieties, one of the most popular, the chickpea or garbanzo, was actually brought over by the Spaniards. Chickpeas have been a Mediterranean staple since the slaves building the Great Pyramid of Cheops were fed on them daily, around 3000 B.C.

This simple fish and vegetable sauté is a substantial, quick meal-in-a-pan. Garbanzos and spinach make an excellent combination.

**Makes 4 to 6 servings**

**1 whole red snapper, cleaned**

**1 tablespoon fresh lime juice**

**Pinch of ground cumin**

**Pinch of saffron threads**

**Kosher salt and freshly ground black pepper to taste**

**3 tablespoons vegetable oil**

**12 shiitake mushrooms, stems removed and caps sliced 1/4 inch thick**

**2 red bell peppers, roasted (page 6), peeled, seeded, and diced**

**1 teaspoon chopped fresh thyme leaves**

**1 tablespoon finely chopped shallot**

**3 cups Fish Stock (page 33)**

**2 cups drained freshly cooked or canned garbanzos**

**8 ounces fresh spinach, well washed and tough stems removed**

**1 tablespoon finely chopped cilantro leaves**

**Marinate the whole** snapper in the lime juice, cumin, and saffron for 10 minutes in a glass dish.

In a large skillet with a lid, heat the oil over medium-high heat. Add the fish and cook, turning once, just until the surfaces have browned. Add the mushrooms, red peppers, thyme, and shallot, reduce the heat to medium, and cook until the vegetables soften, about 5 minutes. Shake the skillet occasionally to prevent the fish from sticking. Pour the stock into the skillet, add the garbanzos, season with salt and pepper, and cover. Cook until the fish is just cooked through and the garbanzos are heated through, 10 to 15 minutes. Uncover the skillet, add the spinach, and stir gently until wilted. Serve immediately, making a bed of garbanzos and vegetables on a large serving plate and resting a fillet on top. Spoon some cooking liquid over and sprinkle with cilantro.

# Fish Baked in Fresh Tangerine Juice and Parsley

*Makes 6 servings*

**Unsalted butter, corn oil, or nonstick spray for greasing the baking dish**

**3 pounds red snapper or striped bass fillets, skin on**

**2 tablespoons freshly squeezed lemon juice**

**1 ½ teaspoons kosher salt**

**1 teaspoon freshly ground black pepper**

**1 tablespoon olive oil**

**1 tablespoon unsalted butter, melted**

**¼ pound button mushrooms, sliced**

**1 tablespoon chopped fresh parsley leaves**

**1 scallion, white and pale green parts, thinly sliced**

**1 cup dry white wine**

**½ cup freshly squeezed tangerine juice (orange or peach juice make good substitutes if tangerine is unavailable)**

Seafood and citrus are a classic combination in many world cuisines, but lemon and lime are certainly more common than tangerine! The sunny sweetness of fresh tangerine juice blends beautifully with the woodsy mushrooms, green parsley, and tender white fish in this recipe. This bright-tasting, low-fat entree from Brazil is great with a substantial grain dish such as Sweet Plantain Rice (page 168) or Roasted Corn and Garlic Rice (page 169).

**Preheat the oven** to 400 degrees. Lightly grease a medium-size glass or ceramic baking dish and arrange the fish fillets in it in layers. In a small glass or ceramic bowl, combine the lemon juice, salt, pepper, oil, and melted butter and pour over the fish. Top with the mushrooms, parsley, and scallion. Pour on the wine and tangerine juice. Bake, uncovered, until the fish is barely opaque, 10 to 20 minutes, depending on the thickness of the fillets. Serve immediately.

# Sea Bass and Saffron Risotto

Makes 4 servings

**3 cups Fish Stock (page 33)**

**3 cups boiling water**

**2 tablespoons unsalted butter**

**2 medium-size shallots, minced**

**2 cups arborio rice, rinsed**

**¼ cup dry, light white wine such as Pinot Grigio**

**½ teaspoon saffron threads**

**12 ounces sea bass fillets, skin removed and cut into ½-inch dice**

**1 tablespoon freshly grated Romano cheese**

**2 small ripe plum tomatoes, seeded and finely diced**

**1 tablespoon freshly chopped chives**

$R$isotto may seem a quintessentially Italian preparation, but soupy, flavorful stews of rice, vegetables, herbs, and fish are popular all over Latin America. Like risottos, these dishes—such as *arroz con camarones* (rice with shrimp) and *arroz con pollo* (rice with chicken)—are named in honor of the grain rather than the flavorings. Pacific sea bass, known as *corvina,* is a sweet, firm fish, used frequently in Chilean and Peruvian cooking. Serve with Gratin of Hearts of Palm (page 173).

**Combine the stock** and water in a medium-size saucepan over low heat.

In a medium-size heavy nonreactive saucepan, melt the butter. Add the shallots and cook over medium heat, stirring, until softened, about 5 minutes. Add the rice and stir to coat. Add the wine and saffron and cook until it is all absorbed by the rice. Add a ladleful of stock and cook, stirring, until it is all absorbed by the rice. Add another ladleful of stock and continue cooking in the same manner, adding stock only as needed and stirring frequently, until rice is tender, about 25 minutes. When the rice has been cooking for 15 minutes, add the fish to the pot and continue cooking just until the rice and fish are cooked through. Just before serving, stir in the cheese, tomatoes, and chives. Serve immediately.

# Baked Cod with *Tomaticán*

Makes 4 servings

**1 tablespoon unsalted butter**

**Four 6- to 8-ounce cod fillets, ½ to ¾ inch thick**

**1 cup dry white wine**

**Kosher salt and freshly ground black pepper to taste**

**2 tablespoons seeded and diced ripe plum tomatoes**

**2 teaspoons finely chopped scallions, white and pale green parts**

**4 large eggs, lightly beaten**

**1 teaspoon chopped cilantro leaves**

When an Argentinian sous-chef I worked with first told me about this dish, I thought that the combination sounded a bit . . . strange. Fish and scrambled eggs? I'm so glad I tried it, because it's become one of my family's favorite fast dinners. Highly seasoned with tomato, scallion, and cilantro, scrambled eggs take on new dimensions as a sauce for firm, flaky cod—and get a new name, *tomaticán*. You could add a bit of minced fresh hot pepper along with the scallions if you like. Serve with Cartagena Coconut-Pineapple Rice (page 170).

**Preheat the oven** to 400 degrees. Use 1 teaspoon of the butter to grease a glass or ceramic baking dish just large enough to hold the fillets in a single layer. Arrange the fillets in the dish, add the wine, and sprinkle with salt and pepper. Bake just until opaque and firm, 10 to 20 minutes, depending on the thickness of the fillets.

Meanwhile, melt the remaining 2 teaspoons butter in a small nonreactive skillet over medium heat. Add the tomatoes and scallions and cook, stirring, until softened, about 3 minutes. Add the eggs, reduce the heat to medium-low, and cook, stirring constantly, until the eggs just come together. Sprinkle with the cilantro, season with salt and pepper, stir, and serve on top of the cod.

## Martha's Black Bean and Lobster Risotto

3 cups Fish Stock (page 33)

3 cups boiling water

2 tablespoons unsalted butter

2 scallions, white and pale green parts,
    finely chopped

2 cups arborio rice, rinsed

¼ cup dry, light white wine such as
    Pinot Grigio

⅔ cup drained freshly cooked
    (page 3) or canned black beans

2 lobster tails, fresh or thawed frozen,
    shelled, meat sliced ¼ inch thick, or
    1 pound peeled and deveined large
    shrimp, sliced ½ inch thick

¾ cup fresh or thawed frozen small
    green peas

1 tablespoon freshly grated Romano
    cheese

2 small ripe plum tomatoes, seeded
    and finely diced

A new take on black beans and rice, with sweet chunks of lobster, tomatoes, and scallions to lighten and flavor the mixture. I invented this dish as a treat for my wife, who loves risotto. Serve with Gratin of Hearts of Palm (page 173).

Combine the stock and water in a medium-size saucepan over low heat.

In a medium-size, heavy saucepan, melt the butter. Add the scallions and cook over medium heat, stirring, until softened, about 5 minutes. Add the rice and stir to coat. Add the wine and cook until it is all absorbed by the rice. Add a ladleful of stock and cook, stirring, until it is all absorbed by the rice. Add another ladleful of stock and continue cooking in the same manner, adding stock only as needed and stirring frequently, until the rice is tender, about 25 minutes. When the rice has been cooking for 15 minutes, add the beans to the pot. Five minutes later, stir in the lobster and peas. Continue cooking just until the rice and lobster are cooked through. Just before serving, stir in the cheese and tomatoes. Serve immediately.

# Shrimp and Lobster Hash Browns

When I was the chef at a large, bustling restaurant called Metropolis, we served hundreds of New Yorkers brunch every Sunday. I noticed that whatever else people chose, they all wanted our savory, crisp hash browns alongside. I thought—why not make hash browns the main attraction? With the addition of delicate shrimp, fresh corn, and cilantro, the flavors are as wonderful for a light summer family dinner as for friends at a leisurely brunch.

Makes 4 servings

12 medium-size shrimp in their shells

1 tablespoon olive oil

2 cups water

2 large Idaho potatoes, peeled and cut into ½-inch dice

3 tablespoons unsalted butter

3 scallions, white and pale green parts, chopped

1 ripe plum tomato, seeded and chopped

2 tablespoons coarsely chopped cilantro leaves

½ cup fresh or frozen corn kernels

Kosher salt and freshly ground black pepper to taste

1 pound lump lobster or crabmeat, picked over for cartilage and shells

**Peel the shrimp,** reserving the shells. Devein the shrimp, if necessary, and refrigerate. In a saucepan, heat the oil over medium-high heat. Add the shrimp shells and cook, stirring occasionally, for 3 minutes, then add the water and bring to a boil. Reduce the heat to medium-low and simmer, uncovered, until reduced by half, about 30 minutes. Strain out the shells and keep the stock hot.

Meanwhile, bring a medium-size saucepan of water to a boil and add the potatoes. Cook until just tender, about 10 minutes, and drain. Slice the raw shrimp into ½-inch lengths.

In a large nonreactive skillet, melt the butter over medium heat. Add the scallions, tomato, cilantro, and corn, season with salt and pepper, and cook, stirring, until softened, about 3 minutes. Add the potatoes, increase the heat to medium-high, and cook, stirring, until the mixture is dry and beginning to brown, about 2 minutes. Add the stock and heat through. Add the shrimp and cook, stirring, until cooked through, about 2 minutes. Add the lobster or crabmeat and heat through. Season with salt and pepper and serve immediately.

# New World Paella (Paella Nuevo Mundo)

*Makes 4 servings*

**1 tablespoon olive oil**

**2 teaspoons finely minced garlic**

**2 cups long-grain rice, rinsed**

**2 pinches of saffron threads**

**2 pinches of sazón Goya (page 6)**

**5 cups Fish Stock (page 33), at room temperature, or salted water**

**2 pinches of kosher salt**

**3 tablespoons seeded and diced ripe tomato**

**8 large littleneck clams, cleaned as described on page 102**

**12 mussels, cleaned as described for clams on page 102**

**2 dry chorizos (page 3), diced**

*T*his *paella* just may be the most popular dish at Bistro Latino. I've made it for groups of two to two hundred people, and it's always a tremendous hit. I do use a traditional Spanish *paella* pan, but otherwise this is far from a classic *paella*. Instead of short-grain Valencia, I like to use long-grain rice to lighten the texture of the dish. The chunks of cured chorizo lend flavor and heat. Sprinkling black beans and *hogo* over the top at the end of the cooking makes the dish beautiful, impressive, and very New World—hence *Nuevo Mundo*.

*Paella* is an essentially simple dish, without complicated seasonings, but it's important to follow the steps of the recipe carefully so that everything cooks together. From start to finish, the whole cooking process should take no more than 30 minutes. This recipe can be multiplied for as many people as you like. The lobster adds wonderful briny flavor and sweet meat, but it must be quartered while still alive—so I've made it optional in deference to the squeamish.

**In a large nonreactive skillet** with curved sides, heat the oil over medium heat. Add the garlic and cook, stirring, until softened, about 2 minutes. Add the rice and stir until each grain is completely coated with oil. Sprinkle the saffron and sazón over the rice and stir. Add 3 cups of the stock and a pinch of salt to the skillet. Bring to a simmer and simmer gently, uncovered, stirring occasionally. After 5 minutes, add the tomato and stir. Simmer 3 minutes more. The mixture should still be quite soupy; as the liquid is absorbed, add more stock ½ cup at a time.

2 small fresh lobsters, about 1¼
   pounds, rinsed and quartered
   (optional; see Note) or additional
   shrimp
8 large shrimp, peeled and deveined
½ cup drained freshly cooked (page 3)
   or canned black beans
2 tablespoons thinly sliced scallions,
   white and pale green parts
¼ cup *Hogo* (page 11)

Place the clams in the skillet, gently pushing them down into the rice. After the clams have cooked for 3 minutes, place the mussels in the skillet, gently pushing them down into the rice. After this point, do not stir the mixture, but move it gently every so often with a wooden spoon to make sure it is not sticking to the pan. Add more liquid only sparingly, keeping in mind that the final product should be quite dry. After the mussels have cooked for about 2 minutes, add the chorizo, pushing the pieces down into the rice. Place the lobsters, if using, and the shrimp on top of the mixture. Cook until the rice is cooked through but not mushy, about 5 minutes more. Sprinkle the *paella* with the black beans and scallions, then drizzle the *hogo* over the top. Serve from the pot at the table.

*Make sure the lobster claws are held together with rubber bands. Wrapping your hand in a kitchen towel, lay a lobster belly down on a steady surface and hold it firmly around the tail. Push the tip of a knife into the flesh between the head and the neck to sever the spinal cord. Let stand 2 minutes. Turn the lobster over and use a large kitchen knife or shears to cut it in half lengthwise. Discard the black vein behind the tail and the stomach sac behind the head. Twist off the claws. You now have four large pieces of lobster. Repeat with the remaining lobster.*

# Shrimp with Coconut Sauce (Camarones al Coco)

*Makes 4 to 6 servings*

**24 large shrimp, peeled and deveined**

**1 small red onion, thinly sliced**

**1 teaspoon finely minced garlic**

**3 tablespoons olive oil**

**1 tablespoon freshly chopped cilantro leaves**

**½ cup cream of coconut, such as Coco Lopez (page 4)**

**1 cup unsweetened coconut milk (page 4)**

**¼ cup pineapple juice**

**2 tablespoons vegetable oil**

**Kosher salt and freshly ground black pepper to taste**

**1 pound mesclun (optional)**

**Chopped fresh chives**

Shrimp and coconut are favorite ingredients of the Caribbean coastal region of Colombia, just two of the many culinary links between mainland Latin America and the islands. It's a combination that immediately transports you to the tropics, even if the shrimp are from your local fish market and the coconut milk comes in a can. The coconut sauce for the shrimp isn't cooked; coconut milk tastes best at room temperature. For a green vegetable, wilt some mesclun in the same pan you use to cook the shrimp. Serve with white rice or Sweet Plantain Rice (page 168).

**In a large bowl,** combine the shrimp, onion, garlic, olive oil, and cilantro. Toss well, cover, refrigerate, and let marinate for 30 minutes.

In a large glass or ceramic bowl, combine the cream of coconut, coconut milk, and pineapple juice.

In a large skillet, heat the vegetable oil over high heat. Lift the shrimp and onion out of the marinade and add them to the skillet. Cook, stirring, just until the shrimp are pink and cooked through and the onion has softened, about 3 minutes. Transfer to the bowl with the coconut mixture and mix gently to coat. Season with salt and pepper. If using mesclun, reheat the skillet, add the mesclun, sprinkle with salt and pepper, and toss over medium heat until wilted. Divide on serving plates. Serve with the shrimp and coconut sauce, sprinkled with chives.

# Rice Simmered with Chicken and Chorizo (*Arroz con Pollo*)

*Makes 2 servings*

**2 tablespoons olive oil**

**8 ounces boneless, skinless chicken breast, preferably free range, cut crosswise into ½-inch strips**

**1 fresh chorizo (page 3), sliced ¼ inch thick**

**1 teaspoon minced garlic**

**1 small white onion, diced**

**1 cup long-grain rice, rinsed**

**2½ cups Chicken Stock (page 32), canned low-sodium chicken broth, or salted water**

**¼ teaspoon sazón Goya (page 6)**

**1 bay leaf**

**1 carrot, sliced ¼ inch thick**

**½ cup fresh or frozen corn kernels**

**½ cup fresh or frozen green peas**

**Kosher salt and freshly ground black pepper to taste**

**1 red bell pepper, roasted (page 6), peeled, seeded, and sliced into strips, or storebought roasted pepper strips**

**Chopped fresh chives**

This recipe, in many different regional guises, may be the single most popular dish in Latin America and the Caribbean. It's easy to see why: *Arroz con pollo,* or rice with chicken, is filling, comforting, healthy, and easy. It's real comfort food, and I especially like it with chorizo added for spice and seasoning.

**In a large, heavy skillet** with a lid, heat the oil over medium-high heat. Add the chicken, chorizo, garlic, and onion and cook, stirring occasionally, until the meats have browned, about 5 minutes. Add the rice and stir until evenly coated with oil. Add the stock, sazón, bay leaf, and carrot and stir. Cover tightly, bring to a simmer, and reduce the heat to very low. Cook for 15 minutes, then sprinkle the corn and peas on top of the rice. Put the lid on the pot and continue to cook until the rice is cooked through and all the liquid is absorbed, 5 to 10 minutes more. Keep covered until ready to serve. Just before serving, season with salt and pepper, mix gently with a fork, and lay the red pepper strips on top. Serve sprinkled with chives.

## Chicken Breasts Stuffed with Chorizo, Goat Cheese, and Scallions

Delicate chicken breasts are the perfect foil for a spicy, flavorful stuffing. This one gets its big taste from just three ingredients: goat cheese, scallions, and chorizo. Chorizo is a fresh, spicy pork sausage common in Spanish, Portuguese, and Latin cooking, though it is a little different in each incarnation (see page 3). If you can't find chorizo for this recipe, cook a pound of hot Italian bulk sausage with a teaspoon of cumin seeds in a skillet until brown, then pour off the fat and add the scallions to the skillet to make the stuffing. I often serve slices of this as an appetizer—the spiral design is attractive over greens—but it also makes a great entree with a tomato or avocado salad and a hot potato dish like Colombian Potatoes with Hot Cheese Sauce (page 162).

Makes 4 servings

2 teaspoons olive oil

¾ pound fresh chorizo, sliced ¼ inch thick

3 scallions, white and pale green parts, finely chopped

4 large boneless, skinless chicken breast halves, preferably free range

8 ounces fresh soft goat cheese, crumbled

Kosher salt and freshly ground black pepper to taste

**In a small skillet,** heat the oil over medium heat and cook the chorizo and scallions, stirring, until brown, 3 to 5 minutes. Remove from the heat and let cool for 10 minutes.

Meanwhile, one by one, place the chicken breasts between two sheets of plastic wrap and roll with a rolling pin or a wine bottle, pressing down, to reduce them to a uniform ¼-inch thickness. Spoon one quarter of the sausage mixture in a line along one side of each chicken breast. Place one quarter of the goat cheese in a parallel line about ¼ inch away. Starting at the end with the chorizo and cheese, roll each breast tightly and wrap securely in plastic wrap.

Meanwhile, bring a saucepan of water large enough to hold the roulades in one layer to a simmer. Poach the wrapped roulades for 10 minutes, then remove with tongs and let cool. When cool enough to handle, unwrap and, using a very sharp knife, cut into ½-inch-thick slices. (Or chill in the plastic wrap until ready to serve, then slice just before serving.) Sprinkle the slices with salt and pepper and serve.

## Peruvian Roast Chicken with Purple Potatoes

*Makes 4 servings*

**For the chicken:**

1 small bunch cilantro, roots and stems discarded

1 teaspoon chopped fresh thyme leaves

2 tablespoons soy sauce

3 tablespoons vegetable oil

1 tablespoon chipotle puree (page 3) or 1 whole chipotle in *adobo*

1 teaspoon honey

¾ cup lager beer

One 3-pound fresh chicken, preferably free range

**For the potatoes:**

2 pounds purple or other small roasting potatoes

1 small garlic clove, minced

1 tablespoon olive oil

1 teaspoon chopped fresh thyme leaves

Kosher salt and freshly ground black pepper to taste

Roast chicken is one Peruvian dish that has made a very happy transition to the States, judging from the proliferation of restaurants dedicated to that dish in New York City alone. It's the soy sauce and honey in the glaze that give the chicken excellent color and flavor. Soy sauce (known in Latin America as *salsa negra*, or black sauce) is very common in Peruvian cooking, thanks to the Asian immigrants who have contributed much to the Peruvian pantry since their arrival in the nineteenth century. Peruvian potatoes—starchier and more colorful than American ones—have also become widely available here, and this is a perennially popular entree at Bistro Latino. Roasting the potatoes retains the deep purple color more effectively than boiling or steaming, and it's so easy just to toss them into the pan with the chicken.

**In a blender or food processor,** combine the cilantro, thyme, soy sauce, 2 tablespoons of the oil, the chipotle, honey, and beer and process until smooth. Rub the chicken with this mixture inside and out, cover with plastic wrap, and refrigerate for 30 minutes.

Preheat the oven to 350 degrees. In a heavy roasting pan or large skillet, combine the potatoes, garlic, oil, thyme, salt, and pepper and toss to coat evenly. Place the chicken, legs down, on top of the potatoes. Rub a sheet of aluminum foil with the remaining tablespoon oil and use it to cover the chicken, oiled side down. Roast for 1 hour, then remove the foil and roast until the skin is golden and the leg joint moves easily in the socket, another 15 to 20 minutes. Remove the chicken to a platter, cover with foil, and stir the potatoes in the pan. Return the potatoes to the oven and keep hot while the chicken rests, 5 to 10 minutes. Carve and serve immediately with the potatoes.

## Roast Chicken with Jalapeños and Yuca (*Ají de Pollo*)

An *ají*, in Latin America, is not only a chile pepper but also a dish in which chile pepper is the most important seasoning. (*Ají* was the indigenous name for this lively fruit in the Caribbean; we get the word *chile* from the Toltecs of Mexico.) That's true here, although a traditional *ají* comes out of the stew pot, not a roasting pan. Roasted poblanos provide just the right level of heat (that is, not very much). Pureed, the chiles permeate the flesh of the chicken and create a deliciously fresh-tasting glaze for the skin.

Makes 4 servings

3 jalapeño peppers, roasted (page 6), peeled, and seeded

1½ cups *Hogo* (page 11)

1 bay leaf

One 3-pound fresh chicken, preferably free range

One 24-ounce bag frozen yuca, thawed for 30 minutes at room temperature and tough cores cut out (page 8)

½ envelope sazón Goya (page 6)

3 tablespoons olive oil

**In a blender or food processor,** combine the roasted peppers, *hogo,* and bay leaf and process until smooth. Rub the chicken inside and out with this mixture, cover with plastic wrap, and refrigerate for 30 minutes.

Preheat the oven to 350 degrees. With a heavy knife, slice the yuca ½ inch thick. In a large heavy roasting pan or skillet, toss the yuca with the sazón and 2 tablespoons of the oil until evenly coated. Shake the pan to spread the yuca evenly over the bottom. Place the chicken, legs down, on top of the yuca. Rub a sheet of aluminum foil with the remaining tablespoon oil and use it to cover the chicken, oiled side down. Roast 1 hour, then remove the foil and roast until the skin is golden and the leg joint moves easily in the socket, another 15 to 20 minutes. Remove the chicken to a platter, cover with foil, and stir the yuca in the pan. Return the yuca to the oven and keep hot while the chicken rests, 5 to 10 minutes more. Carve and serve immediately with the yuca.

# Roast Turkey with Chorizo-Apple-Cornbread Stuffing

Makes 8 to 10 servings

1½ cups coarse-ground cornmeal, preferably stone ground

½ cup all-purpose flour

2½ teaspoons baking powder

1 tablespoon sugar

¾ teaspoon kosher salt

1 large egg

2 tablespoons unsalted butter, melted

1 cup whole or 2% milk

½ cup (1 stick) unsalted butter

1 medium-size red onion, thinly sliced

2 scallions, white and pale green parts, thinly sliced

2 firm, not-too-sweet apples, such as Granny Smith or Golden Delicious

3 dry chorizos (page 3), cut into ¼-inch dice

¼ cup chopped fresh parsley leaves

1½ cups fresh or frozen corn kernels

Cooks in the United States take the turkey for granted most of the year, but when it was introduced to France in the sixteenth century, the new bird created a sensation on the tables of the aristocracy. It was the first "new" fowl to be introduced to European cuisine since Roman times, and Louis XIV himself obtained a private flock, complete with an honorary Captain of the Royal Turkeys to take care of the precious, if ugly, birds. We tend to think of the turkey as an all-American bird, but in its indigenous Latin America, under the name of *pavo*, it is the centerpiece of classics like Oaxacan *mole poblano* and countless *pavo guisado*, or stewed turkey dishes. This makes a festive autumn or winter dish; using a smaller turkey means better flavor, faster cooking, and fewer leftovers.

**Make the cornbread:** Preheat the oven to 425 degrees. Grease a 9-inch glass or ceramic baking dish and place it to heat in the oven. In a large bowl, combine the cornmeal, flour, baking powder, sugar, and salt. In a small bowl, whisk the egg. Whisk in the melted butter and milk. Rapidly mix the egg mixture into the flour mixture. Scrape the batter into the heated pan and bake until golden brown and a tester comes out clean, 20 to 25 minutes. Set aside to cool. When cool enough to

1 small fresh turkey, preferably free
    range, about 10 pounds
Freshly ground black pepper to taste
1 recipe Mango Barbecue Sauce
    (page 21) or Chipotle-Guava Glaze
    (page 22), or 2 cups (4 sticks) butter,
    melted, for basting

handle, cut or crumble into ¾-inch chunks and place in a large bowl.

Make the stuffing: In a skillet, melt the ½ cup of butter over medium-high heat. Add the onion, scallions, and apples and cook, stirring, until softened, 5 to 8 minutes. Add the chorizos, parsley, and corn and cook, stirring, just until heated through. Add to the cornbread and mix well. Set aside to cool to room temperature or refrigerate.

Preheat the oven to 450 degrees. Rinse the turkey well and pat it dry, then season it inside and out with salt and pepper. Stuff the cavity with the stuffing, packing loosely. With long skewers, skewer the opening shut, and secure the legs in place. Place the turkey, legs up, on a rack in a shallow roasting pan. Baste the turkey with sauce, glaze, or butter and place a tent of aluminum foil over the breast. Place in the oven legs first, and reduce the heat to 350 degrees. Roast 2½ to 3 hours, basting every hour for the first two hours of cooking, then every twenty minutes or so. Remove the foil for the last 45 minutes of cooking.

When the juices run clear from the thigh and the internal temperature of the stuffing is about 165 degrees, remove the turkey from the oven, cover with foil, and let rest for 20 minutes. Meanwhile, place a serving platter in the oven to heat. Remove the stuffing to a serving bowl. Carve the turkey and serve as soon as possible.

# Chilean Stir-Fried Pork (*Chancho a la Chileña*)

*Makes 3 to 4 servings*

3 tablespoons vegetable or peanut oil

1 pound boneless pork loin or shoulder, trimmed of fat and cut into ¾-inch dice

1 large red onion, diced

2 garlic cloves, minced

4 ripe plum tomatoes, diced

1½ cups Chicken Stock (page 32) or canned low-sodium chicken broth

2 teaspoons distilled white vinegar

Kosher salt and freshly ground black pepper to taste

¼ cup chopped fresh parsley leaves

This easy vinegar-spiked sauté is a Chilean favorite—so much so that when I called the Chilean consulate in New York for an authentic recipe, no fewer than three helpful people insisted on giving me their version. Serve over white rice or Roasted Corn and Garlic Rice (page 169) to soak up the savory sauce.

**In a large nonreactive skillet,** heat the oil over high heat. Add the pork dice and brown on all sides, 10 to 12 minutes. Add the onion, garlic, and tomatoes and cook for 2 minutes. Add the stock and vinegar, season with salt and pepper, and cook until the liquid thickens to a sauce, 5 to 10 minutes. Serve over rice, sprinkled with the parsley.

# Colombian Rice with Pork Loin, Potatoes, and Herbs (*Arroz Atollado*)

*Makes 8 to 10 servings*

**3 quarts water**

**2 bay leaves**

**1 tablespoon kosher salt**

**2 pounds pork short ribs, trimmed of fat and cut into 1-inch lengths (have the butcher do this for you)**

**½ pound pork loin, trimmed of fat and cut into ¾-inch dice**

**1 pound fresh chorizo (page 3), sliced ½ inch thick**

**1½ cups *Hogo* (page 11)**

**3 cups long-grain rice, rinsed**

**¼ cup olive oil**

**1 tablespoon black peppercorns**

**½ teaspoon ground white pepper**

This robust dish of the Colombian Andes makes a great fall or winter dinner. Rice and potatoes, an unusual combination, are great when pulled together with a savory *hogo,* two kinds of pepper, and fresh herbs.

**In a large, heavy pot** with a tight-fitting lid, combine the water, bay leaves, 2 teaspoons of salt, and both kinds of pork. Bring to a boil, reduce the heat to medium-low, and simmer for 30 minutes.

Meanwhile, in a medium-size skillet, brown the chorizo over high heat. Drain on paper towels.

Add the browned chorizo, half of the *hogo,* the rice, and oil to the broth. Add 1 teaspoon salt, the peppercorns, and white pepper and simmer, uncovered, for 20 minutes, stirring occasionally. Add the potatoes and

1 pound purple or other starchy
　potatoes, peeled and cut into
　½-inch dice
1 cup fresh or frozen green peas
2 tablespoons finely chopped cilantro
　leaves
2 tablespoons finely chopped fresh
　parsley leaves
2 tablespoons thinly sliced scallions,
　white and pale green parts
4 hard-boiled eggs (optional), peeled
　and diced

peas, stir, reduce the heat to very low, and cover tightly. Cook (do not stir) until the rice and potatoes are cooked through, about 20 minutes. The rice should remain moist; add a small amount of boiling water if necessary. Just before serving, add half the cilantro, half the parsley, half the scallions, and the diced eggs, if using, and stir gently with a fork. Serve in heated plates, sprinkled with the remaining herbs and scallions and topped with a spoonful of *hogo*.

# Tía Donna's Colombian Tamales

*Makes 6 large tamales*

**12 ounces boneless, skinless chicken thighs, preferably free range, cut into ½-inch dice**

**12 ounces pork shoulder, butt, or loin, trimmed of fat and cut into ½-inch dice**

**12 ounces pork short ribs, trimmed of fat and cut into 1-inch lengths (have the butcher do this for you)**

**⅓ cup olive oil**

**1 teaspoon sazón Goya (page 6)**

**Kosher salt and freshly ground black pepper to taste**

**2 cups fine-ground cornmeal**

**2 cups hot Chicken Stock (page 32) or canned low-sodium chicken broth**

**1 teaspoon roasted garlic (page 6)**

**6 fresh or frozen banana leaves or sheets of parchment paper, about 12 × 15 inches each**

Making tamales is a family affair, as I discovered the night Aunt Donna decided it was time to teach my daughter, Amanda—then three years old—the rudiments of *tamal*-making. Amanda loved patting out the dough, counting the garbanzos and capers for each *tamal,* and wrapping the finished product in shiny green banana leaves. If you have plenty of helpers, multiply this recipe by three or four and throw a *tamalada*—a *tamal*-making party. After the steaming, simply freeze leftover tamales in plastic bags. They last indefinitely, and my Aunt Donna insists that the flavor actually improves over time. To reheat, place the frozen tamales in a steamer and steam until heated through.

**The day before** you plan to serve the tamales, combine the chicken, both kinds of pork, oil, and sazón in a large bowl and season with salt and pepper. Mix well, cover, and marinate overnight, stirring occasionally.

Place the cornmeal in a large bowl and add the stock and garlic. Mix until the mixture holds together and is faintly sticky to the touch, adding boiling water if needed to moisten the dough. Let rest, covered, for 10 minutes.

*tamales*

**6 long, thin strips banana leaf or**
  **kitchen string for tying**

**3 scallions, white and pale green**
  **parts, thinly sliced**

**1 large carrot, sliced ¼ inch thick**

**3 small new potatoes, quartered**
  **(peeling is optional)**

**24 freshly cooked or canned**
  **garbanzos (chickpeas)**

**12 capers**

**6 pimento-stuffed olives**

***Ají* (optional; page 9)**

Wipe a banana leaf clean with a clean, damp kitchen cloth and lay it lengthwise on your work surface, with the grain running from left to right. Divide the dough evenly into twelve parts. Place one of them in the palm of your hand (your left if you are a righty; your right if you are a lefty) and use the other hand to pat the dough down evenly, spreading it gradually into a pancake that covers your hand. Set aside and repeat with another piece of dough.

Cupping one pancake gently in your hand, place one sixth of the meat filling in the center. Add one sixth of the scallions, one sixth of the carrot, two pieces of potato, four chickpeas, and two capers. Cover with the other pancake and use your fingers to press the dough together around the edges, sealing the filling inside.

Carefully place the *tamal* in the center of the banana leaf. Top with an olive, pressing it gently into the *tamal.* As if wrapping a present, fold the top edge of the banana leaf down over the *tamal,* then fold the bottom up to cover. Fold the ends into the center and turn the *tamal* over. Again as if wrapping a present, tie the *tamal* securely closed. Repeat with the remaining dough, filling, and wrappers.

Arrange a steamer in a large pot with a tight-fitting lid filled with a couple of inches of water. Bring the water to a boil (it should not touch the steamer), place the tamales in the steamer, and steam until cooked through and firm, about 90 minutes. Serve still wrapped and let your guests carefully cut the tamales open at the table. Pass *ají* at the table if desired.

# Colombian Pot Roast (*Sobrebarriga Bogotano*)

Makes 10 to 12 servings

**6 pounds flank steak, preferably with
   some surface fat**

**3 garlic cloves, minced**

**2 medium-size white onions, coarsely
   chopped**

**1 bay leaf**

**2 envelopes sazón Goya (page 6)**

**1 tablespoon olive oil**

**12 ounces lager beer**

**3 cups water**

**Kosher salt and freshly ground black
   pepper to taste**

**Chopped fresh parsley leaves**

**Chopped cilantro leaves**

A specialty of Bogotá—and of the Palomino family. My father seizes every special-occasion opportunity to make *sobrebarriga:* holidays, Sunday dinners, birthdays. And no wonder; his is the best I've ever had. It's a simple dish—in the States we would generally call it a "pot roast," but the lengthy marination and last-minute broiling make this recipe especially succulent and crusty. Before you begin, note that the meat must be marinated at least two days before cooking. In Colombia, *sobrebarriga* is invariably served with *papas chorreadas*—Colombian Potatoes with Hot Cheese Sauce (page 162)—and fresh *ají* (page 9).

**Rinse the steak** under cold running water for 3 minutes, then pat dry and place on a glass or ceramic platter.

In a food processor or blender, combine the garlic, onions, bay leaf, sazón, and oil and pulse just until combined but still chunky. Spread the mixture over both sides of the steak. Gently pour the beer over and around

# pot roast

the steak. Cover tightly with plastic wrap and refrigerate undisturbed for at least two and as long as three days.

Transfer the steak and the marinade to a heavy pot with a tight-fitting lid. Add the water, cover, and heat over medium heat. Cook at a simmer just until cooked through but still tender, about 2 hours. During the cooking, add more water as needed to keep the mixture moist. Do not boil the meat, and do not overcook. (The dish can be made through this step up to two days in advance and refrigerated.)

When ready to serve, preheat a broiler for at least 15 minutes. Arrange the meat on a broiler pan, season with salt and pepper, and transfer the liquid to saucepan. Bring to a simmer and reduce until it has the consistency of a sauce. Season with salt and pepper. Broil the meat on both sides just until golden brown, about 5 minutes per side. Slice the meat against the grain about ½ inch thick, arrange on a platter, and pour the sauce over it. Sprinkle each serving with parsley and cilantro.

# Peruvian Stir-Fried Beef with Onions (*Lomo Saltado*)

*Makes 4 servings*

**1½ pounds sirloin steak, trimmed of
fat and cut into ½-inch dice**

**2 tablespoons olive oil**

**4 garlic cloves, minced**

**½ cup chopped fresh parsley leaves**

**¼ cup vegetable oil**

**6 new potatoes (peeling is optional),
sliced ¼ inch thick**

**4 ripe plum tomatoes, seeded and cut
into 1-inch pieces**

**1 Italian frying pepper, seeded and
thinly sliced**

**2 medium-size red onions, thinly sliced**

**1 large bay leaf**

**1 teaspoon chopped fresh thyme leaves**

**2 teaspoons soy sauce, or more to taste**

**2 teaspoons distilled white vinegar, or
more to taste**

**Kosher salt and freshly ground black
pepper to taste**

**½ cup fresh or frozen green peas**

This Peruvian favorite, seasoned with soy sauce, stir-fried over high heat, and served with white rice, is clearly imported from Asia. Chinese workers flocked to Peru in the nineteenth century to work the cotton and sugar plantations, but most fled the dreadful working conditions as soon as they could. They settled in great numbers in Lima, which soon had the largest Chinatown in the New World. *Lomo saltado* is the defining dish of modern Peruvian *criollo* cooking, with its rich mix of indigenous, European, and Asian influences.

**Put the steak** in a medium-size bowl and add the olive oil, three quarters of the garlic, and half of the parsley. Toss to coat and marinate for 30 to 45 minutes.

In a large nonreactive skillet or wok, heat the vegetable oil over high heat. When it is very hot, add the potatoes and cook, stirring occasionally, until golden brown. Lift the potatoes out of the hot oil and drain on paper towels. Reheat the oil over high heat, adding more if necessary to make ¼ cup. Add the meat and its marinade and cook, stirring, just until browned. Add the tomatoes, frying pepper, onions, the remaining garlic, bay leaf, thyme, soy sauce, and vinegar and season with salt and pepper. Cook, stirring constantly, just until softened. At the last minute, add the potatoes, peas, and the remaining parsley to the skillet and toss to heat through. Adjust the seasonings and serve immediately.

# On the Grill
## (*A la Parilla*)

Garlic Shrimp and Pineapple Skewers
(*Pinchos de Camaron y Piña*)

Grilled Swordfish with Cilantro Pesto

Marinated Tuna Steaks with Hot Papaya
Salsa

Barbecued Ribs with Citrus Marmalade

Beef Skewers (*Pinchos de Carne*)

Grilled Steak Marinated in Citrus (*Palomilla*)

Grilled Steak with Tomato-Onion Relish
(*Bistec ala Criolla*)

Onion-Chile Marinated Sirloin with
*Chimichurri*

Grilled Plantains Stuffed with Guava

## Garlic Shrimp and Pineapple Skewers (*Pinchos de Camaron y Piña*)

*Makes 4 to 8 servings*

**24 jumbo shrimp, peeled and deveined**

**¾ cup olive oil**

**3 garlic cloves, minced**

**1 tablespoon finely chopped cilantro leaves**

**8 ounces guava paste (page 4)**

**¼ cup water**

**1 shallot, finely minced**

**2 teaspoons chipotle puree (page 3), or more to taste**

**2 cups peeled fresh pineapple chunks**

These sweet, smoky, "shrimpy" skewers make great party food. You can marinate the shrimp and assemble the skewers well in advance, then briefly grill them just before serving—or up to two hours ahead. Serve with Cartagena Coconut–Pineapple Rice (page 170).

**If using wooden skewers,** put them to soak in plenty of water for about 30 minutes. Combine the shrimp, oil, and garlic in a large bowl, mix well, and let marinate for 1 hour in the refrigerator. Place the cilantro, guava paste, water, shallot, and chipotle puree in a blender or food processor and process until smooth. Transfer to a large glass or ceramic bowl. Lift the shrimp out of the oil and add to the guava mixture. Add the pineapple and mix well. Marinate for another 5 to 10 minutes. Do not overmarinate or the shrimp will become mushy.

Alternating with chunks of pineapple, thread the shrimp onto the skewers, folding each shrimp in half and pushing the point through both ends. Transfer the marinade to a small saucepan and simmer briefly.

Meanwhile, heat a grill to very hot. Grill the skewers just until the shrimp are cooked through, about 2 minutes per side, basting frequently with the marinade. Serve immediately or at room temperature.

## Grilled Swordfish with Cilantro Pesto

Makes 4 to 6 servings

¼ cup olive oil

2 teaspoons minced garlic

½ teaspoon ground cumin

1 cup lager beer

Four to six 6- to 8-ounce swordfish steaks, about ¾ inch thick

Kosher salt and freshly ground black pepper to taste

¾ cup Cilantro Pesto (page 19)

Since swordfish steaks can be firm and sometimes dry when grilled, an unctuous sauce is called for. The flavors of cumin and beer enhance the natural meatiness of swordfish, and the green herb sauce brightens everything up. Serve with Peruvian Potatoes with Spicy Cheese Sauce (page 163).

**In a large glass** or ceramic baking dish, whisk together the oil, garlic, cumin, and beer. Arrange the swordfish steaks in a single layer in the dish, turn to coat both sides, and cover. Let marinate for 30 minutes in the refrigerator, turning once.

Meanwhile, heat a grill to very hot. Lift the steaks out of the marinade and grill until just cooked through, 3 to 4 minutes per side. Remove from the grill and season with salt and pepper. Top each steak with 2 tablespoons cilantro pesto and serve immediately.

# Marinated Tuna Steaks with Hot Papaya Salsa

Makes 4 to 6 servings

½ cup vegetable oil

1 tablespoon soy sauce

1 tablespoon chopped cilantro leaves

2 garlic cloves, chopped

Four to six 6- to 8-ounce tuna steaks

Kosher salt and freshly ground black
   pepper to taste

1 recipe Hot Papaya Salsa (page 16)

Fruit salsas and grilled fish are an inspired combination, one of my favorite food trends of recent years. Papaya, which has great flavor but usually needs something acidic to spark it up, is particularly suited to salsas with tart citrus and chile heat. Serve with Sweet Plantain Rice (page 168).

**In a blender or food processor,** combine the oil, soy sauce, cilantro, and garlic and process until smooth. Transfer to a large glass or ceramic baking dish, add the tuna steaks in a single layer, turning to coat both sides, and cover. Let marinate in the refrigerator for 30 minutes.

Meanwhile, heat a grill to very hot. Lift the steaks out of the marinade and grill until just cooked through, 3 to 4 minutes per side. Remove from the grill and season with salt and pepper. Top each steak with 2 tablespoons papaya salsa and serve immediately.

# Barbecued Ribs with Citrus Marmalade

Makes 4 servings

**4 slabs pork short ribs, about 1¼ pounds each**

**2 bay leaves**

**1 tablespoon vegetable oil**

**1 medium-size red onion, chopped**

**1 garlic clove, minced**

**1 fresh poblano chile, seeded and minced**

**1 teaspoon ground cinnamon**

**2 tablespoons firmly packed *panela* (page 5) or dark brown sugar**

**1 teaspoon kosher salt**

**1½ teaspoons chipotle puree (page 3)**

**1 quart freshly squeezed orange juice**

*T*his marmalade is so good that I could eat it with a spoon—if I do say so myself. Pork and orange have a natural flavor affinity, often reflected in the cuisines of Cuba, Brazil, and Mexico. This is easier than most other rib recipes: Since the precooking takes place on the stove, there's no need to stand over the grill for hours. Serve with Whipped Potatoes with Black Beans (page 158).

**Place the ribs** in a large pot and cover with salted water. Add the bay leaves and turn the heat to high. Bring to a simmer, reduce the heat, and simmer for one hour and 30 minutes. Drain the ribs and set aside to cool in a large ceramic or glass baking dish.

Meanwhile, in a large nonreactive skillet, heat the oil over medium-high heat. Add the onion, garlic, and poblano and cook, stirring, until softened, about 5 minutes. Add the cinnamon, *panela* or brown sugar, salt, and chipotle puree and cook, stirring, until incorporated and heated through. Pour the orange juice into the skillet, bring to a simmer, and cook until thickened and reduced by half. Reserving ½ cup for basting, pour this marinade over the drained ribs and mix to coat well. Marinate in the refrigerator for at least 1 hour or up to 3 hours.

Heat a grill to very hot. Lift the ribs out of the marinade and grill, turning and basting frequently, until glazed and heated through, 10 to 20 minutes.

# Beef Skewers (*Pinchos de Carne*)

Makes 4 servings

½ cup olive oil

2 large garlic cloves, chopped

1 teaspoon chipotle puree (page 3)

¾ cup coarsely chopped cilantro leaves

1 tablespoon soy sauce

1 teaspoon honey

2 pounds 1-inch-thick boneless sirloin steak, trimmed of fat and cut into 1 × 2-inch strips

High in the hills above the plateau city of Bogotá, winding roads are lined with stands selling *pinchos,* beef skewers that are Bogotanos' favorite late-night snack. Families, policemen, young couples on motorcycles, truckers, and groups of teenagers exhilarated from a night out dancing jostle for position and drink a last cold beer while waiting for the savory meat to cook over hot coals. The aroma is incomparable and the view spectacular.

This smoky-sweet marinade produces skewers of simply delicious beef that go well with any starch or salad. With fresh corn grilled in the husk and sprinkled with chile and lime, plus a tomato–cilantro salad, you've got a heavenly dinner that just screams "Summer." Serve with *Batatas* (page 157) and have a round of Pisco Sours (page 53) first, and don't forget to soak the bamboo skewers before threading the meat so they don't burn on the grill.

**If using wooden skewers,** soak them in plenty of water for about 30 minutes. In a small skillet, heat the olive oil over medium-high heat. Cook the garlic briefly, stirring, until golden. Add the chipotle puree, cilantro, soy sauce, and honey, reduce the heat to a simmer, and cook for 3 minutes. Let cool for 15 minutes at room temperature.

In a large shallow bowl, combine the steak and the marinade, mixing thoroughly to coat. Marinate for 15 minutes at room temperature. Meanwhile, heat a grill to very hot. Weave the strips of meat securely onto the skewers, pushing the skewer up and down through the meat as if it were a needle you were using to sew a seam. Grill for 3 minutes, then turn and grill 3 minutes more, then turn again and grill another 1 to 3 minutes, depending on desired doneness.

# Grilled Steak Marinated in Citrus (*Palomilla*)

Makes 4 servings

**Freshly squeezed juice of 1 orange**

**Freshly squeezed juice of 2 limes**

**¾ cup lager beer, preferably dark and toasty, such as Negro Modelo**

**1 medium-size red onion, finely chopped**

**1 teaspoon kosher salt, or more to taste**

**2 pounds boneless sirloin steaks, not more than ½ inch thick, trimmed of fat**

**Freshly ground black pepper to taste**

**Lime wedges**

*I*n my grilled version of a classic Cuban sauté of thin beefsteaks, briefly marinating the steak in citrus juices softens it without sacrificing flavor. Just make sure to grill the steaks very quickly over a very hot fire; since they are thin, they can overcook in an instant. Drizzle on a bit of Braised Garlic–Thyme *Mojo* with Lime (page 20) to tease out the flavors. Serve with *Moros* (page 171) or Whipped Potatoes with Black Beans (page 158).

**In a large glass** or ceramic baking dish, combine the juices, beer, onion, and salt, add the steaks, turn to coat both sides, cover, and let marinate in the refrigerator for 30 minutes.

Meanwhile, heat a grill to very hot. Lift the steaks out of the marinade and grill just until both sides are well browned, 3 to 4 minutes total. Do not overcook; remember that the steaks are very thin. Season with salt and pepper and serve with lime wedges.

# Grilled Steak with Tomato-Onion Relish (*Bistec ala Criolla*)

*Makes 4 servings*

**Four 8-ounce boneless sirloin steaks, ¾ to 1 inch thick, trimmed of fat**

**Kosher salt and freshly ground black pepper to taste**

**2 teaspoons Dijon mustard**

**1 teaspoon ground cumin**

**½ teaspoon red wine vinegar**

**2 tablespoons vegetable oil**

**1 medium-size red onion, diced**

**2 ripe plum tomatoes, diced**

**1 bay leaf**

**A** Colombian classic. As in the United States, *ala criolla* (Creole style) in Colombia usually means that tomatoes, onions, and a certain piquancy infuse the dish. Here hot mustard, rather than chiles, provides the spice. Colombian chefs pride themselves on the complexities of their *cocina criolla* (Creole cuisine) and its delectable synthesis of ingredients, techniques, and seasonings. (See page xiii for more on *cocina criolla*.) This is a popular hearty breakfast at Colombian ranches and truck stops, but it also makes an excellent dinner in your own backyard or dining room. Serve with Colombian Potatoes with Salt and Scallions (page 161).

**Season the steaks** on both sides with salt and pepper. In a large glass or ceramic baking dish, whisk together the mustard, cumin, and vinegar. Place the steaks in the dish, turn to coat both sides, cover, and let marinate in the refrigerator for 1 hour.

Heat a grill to very hot. In a medium-size nonreactive skillet, heat the oil over medium heat. Add the onion, tomatoes, and bay leaf, reduce the heat to a simmer, and cook until the mixture is soft and thick, about 10 minutes. Season with salt and pepper and set aside to cool.

Meanwhile, grill the steaks until done to your liking, 4 to 6 minutes per side. Serve immediately, topped with the tomato-onion relish.

## Onion-Chile Marinated Sirloin with *Chimichurri*

Makes 6 to 8 servings

2 large fresh poblano chiles

2 medium-size white onions, peeled
    and halved

1 bay leaf

1 small bunch cilantro, roots discarded

2 garlic cloves, peeled

1 cup olive oil

Kosher salt and freshly ground black
    pepper to taste

3 pounds boneless sirloin steaks, about
    1¼ inches thick

½ cup *Chimichurri* (page 12)

*I*n Bogotá, my native city, a steakhouse isn't a steakhouse unless there's a pit full of flaming coals smack in the middle of the restaurant, where everyone can watch the action. On my last trip, I visited Casa Brava, a hilltop steakhouse where the meat is simply tossed with chunks of onion, peppers, garlic, and olive oil before cooking. Using a leek for a brush, the chef doused the meat with the marinade as it grilled. That memorable scene was the inspiration for this dish. Instead of thick sauces or compound butters as a topping for steak, Latin American tastes call for cutting the richness of red meat with a spicy, piquant herbal sauce like *chimichurri*. Serve with Potato-Chipotle Gratin (page 159).

**Heat a grill** or large cast-iron skillet until very hot. Roast the chiles, turning with tongs and pressing down to sear the skin, until the skins are blistered and the flesh soft. Transfer to a paper bag to cool and finish cooking, about 15 minutes. Place the onions, cut side down, on the hot grill. Cook, turning occasionally, until well browned and softened. Transfer to a blender or food processor. Peel and seed the chiles with your fingers (do not rinse the chiles) and add the flesh to the blender. Add the bay leaf, cilantro, garlic, and oil and process until very smooth. Season with salt and pepper. In a large baking dish, slather the steaks with the marinade, cover, and refrigerate 4 to 6 hours, turning occasionally.

Heat a grill to very hot. Lift the steaks from the marinade, shaking to remove any excess, and grill until done to your liking, 6 to 8 minutes per side. Transfer to a platter, cover with aluminum foil, and let rest for 5 minutes before serving. Serve with a tablespoon of *chimichurri* on top of each steak.

## Grilled Plantains Stuffed with Guava

Makes 6 servings

3 large, ripe plantains (page 5; do not
    peel)

6 ounces guava paste, sliced ¼ inch
    thick

Vanilla–Brown Sugar Ice Cream
    (page 187) or another ice cream of
    your choice

Getting your backyard grill to the perfect temperature is no easy task, and when the coals are going nicely, it's frustrating to use them only for ten minutes or so. Use that leftover cooking power in a new way—make dessert. You can prepare these plantains in advance and wrap them in aluminum foil; then, when you sit down to eat, toss them on the still-hot grill. They can cook for up to 30 minutes, as long as the fire is not too hot.

**Heat a grill** to medium hot, or make sure the coals from dinner are still hot enough to cook with. Cutting lengthwise, butterfly the plantains from end to end without cutting all the way through to the back. (Picture the way a hot-dog bun is sliced.) Into the openings, stuff the slices of guava paste. Wrap tightly in aluminum foil and place on the grill. Cook until the plantain is soft and the guava paste melted, about 15 minutes. Unwrap, cut in half crosswise, and open each half on a plate. Top with ice cream and serve.

# Side Dishes

Sweet Potato Fries (*Batatas*)

Whipped Potatoes with Black Beans

Potato-Chipotle Gratin

Cumin Fries

Colombian Potatoes with Salt and Scallions
(*Papas Saladas*)

Colombian Potatoes with Hot Cheese Sauce
(*Papas Chorreadas*)

Peruvian Potatoes with Spicy Cheese Sauce
(*Papas a la Huancaina*)

Yuca Fries

Yuca Hash Browns

Crisp Plantain Coins (*Patacones*)

Mashed Sweet Plantains (*Fufu*)

Sweet Plantain Rice

Roasted Corn and Garlic Rice

Cartagena Coconut-Pineapple Rice
(*Arroz con Coco*)

Black Beans and White Rice (*Moros*)

Colombian Red Beans (*Frijoles Rojos*)

Gratin of Hearts of Palm (*Palmitos Gratinados*)

## Sweet Potato Fries (*Batatas*)

*Makes 4 to 6 servings*

**4 large sweet potatoes, peeled and cut into ¼-inch-thick fries or coins**

**6 cups Chicken Stock (page 32), canned low-sodium chicken broth, or salted water**

**Vegetable oil for frying**

**Kosher salt to taste**

**Paprika**

*S*weet potatoes fry up beautifully, especially if they're first simmered in stock to enrich the flavors. This simple preparation is known all over Latin America as *batatas,* the Caribbean Arawak word for sweet potato. These, not white potatoes, were the first potatoes introduced to Europe; Columbus brought them back to Spain from what is now Haiti in 1493. For a spicier effect, use hot paprika or chile powder instead of sweet paprika for sprinkling.

**Place the sweet potatoes** in a large pot, add the stock, cover, and bring to a boil. Boil until softened but still firm, about 10 minutes. Drain and let dry, or pat dry with paper towels.

Preheat the oven to 250 degrees and put an ovenproof serving platter in the oven to heat.

Heat the oil in a deep fryer according to the manufacturer's instructions (or heat 1 inch of oil in a deep pot) to about 365 degrees, hot enough to quickly crisp a test piece of sweet potato. Working in batches if necessary to avoid crowding the pan, fry the sweet potatoes until crisp. As they are cooked, drain them on paper towels, sprinkle lightly with salt and paprika, and keep hot in the oven. Serve immediately.

# Whipped Potatoes with Black Beans

Makes 6 to 8 servings

4 large Idaho potatoes, peeled and
  quartered

6 cups Chicken Stock (page 32), canned
  low-sodium chicken broth, or salted
  water

1 teaspoon kosher salt

1 tablespoon unsalted butter

½ cup heavy cream, at room
  temperature

½ teaspoon roasted garlic (page 6)

1⅓ cups drained freshly cooked
  (page 3) or canned black beans

This savory side dish is a spiced-up alternative to traditional mashed potatoes.

**Place the potatoes** in a large pot, add the stock, cover, and bring to a boil. Let boil until very soft, 20 to 30 minutes. Drain well, then return the potatoes to the pot or transfer to the bowl of an electric mixer fitted with a paddle attachment (don't use the food processor). Add the remaining ingredients and mash until very smooth. If using a hand masher, switch to a sturdy whisk toward the end to help fluff the mixture.

# Potato-Chipotle Gratin

Makes 6 servings

**2 pounds Idaho potatoes, very thinly
   sliced (peeling is optional)**

**1¼ cups *crema agria* (page 4), crème
   fraîche, or heavy cream**

**2 small garlic cloves, minced**

**1 teaspoon chipotle puree (page 3), or
   more to taste**

**1 cup grated Manchego, Gruyère, or
   Swiss cheese**

**2 tablespoons finely chopped cilantro
   leaves or chives**

Perennial favorites in the French kitchen, potato gratins are infinitely adaptable—with or without cream, adding more garlic or less, using ham, herbs, or tomato as flavor accents. In my kitchen, lightly spiced with smoky hot chipotle, potato gratin goes *Nuevo Mundo*.

**Preheat the oven** to 350 degrees.

Arrange half of the potatoes in a greased 6-cup baking dish. In a small bowl, combine the *crema,* garlic, and chipotle puree and mix well. Spread half the mixture evenly over the potatoes. Sprinkle on half the cheese. Repeat with the remaining potatoes, crème fraîche, and cheese. Bake, uncovered, until the potatoes are tender and the top is golden brown, about 1 hour. Check the gratin after 50 minutes; if the top is already brown, cover the dish with aluminum foil for the rest of the baking. Let rest for 10 minutes after baking. Sprinkle with the cilantro and serve.

The earthy, toasty flavor of cumin is a natural accent for potatoes. This technique for frying potatoes—a first cooking at low temperature, followed by a second, hotter, immersion—produces fries of incomparable texture and crispness.

# Cumin Fries

Makes 4 servings

**Vegetable oil for frying**

**4 large Idaho potatoes, peeled if desired, cut into ¼-inch-thick fries, rinsed, and patted dry**

**1 teaspoon ground cumin**

**Kosher salt to taste**

**Heat the oil** in a deep fryer according to the manufacturer's instructions (or heat 3 inches of oil in a deep, heavy pot) to 250 degrees. Working in batches if necessary to avoid crowding the pan, fry the potatoes in the oil until barely golden, about 5 minutes. Remove, drain on paper towels, and let cool at room temperature for at least 10 minutes or up to 3 hours.

When ready to serve, preheat the oven to 250 degrees and put an ovenproof serving platter in the oven to heat.

Reheat the oil to 365 degrees, hot enough to quickly crisp a test piece of potato. Working in batches to avoid crowding the pan, fry the potatoes until deep brown and puffed, 3 to 5 minutes. As they are cooked, drain on paper towels, sprinkle lightly with the cumin and salt, and keep hot in the oven. Serve immediately.

# Colombian Potatoes with Salt and Scallions (*Papas Saladas*)

Makes 6 to 8 servings

**2 pounds small new potatoes, scrubbed**

**6 cups cold water**

**2 tablespoons kosher or sea salt**

**6 scallions, white and pale green parts, very thinly sliced**

This simple recipe is just one of many, many beloved Colombian potato dishes. When you've got your hands on some special small, fresh potatoes from the farmer's market—baby Yukon Golds or fingerlings—give them this treatment. It really sets off the flavor of the potato.

**Combine the potatoes,** water, and 1 tablespoon of the salt in a large pot. Cover, bring to a boil, and cook until the potatoes are very soft, 15 to 20 minutes. Drain the potatoes, return them to the pot, and dry them out over a low flame, shaking the pot. Toss with the remaining tablespoon salt. Mound in a serving bowl and sprinkle thickly with the scallions.

## Colombian Potatoes with Hot Cheese Sauce (Papas Chorreadas)

Makes 10 to 12 servings

**3 pounds medium-size boiling potatoes,
    well washed**

**¼ cup olive oil**

**2 garlic cloves, minced**

**12 scallions, white and pale green
    parts, thinly sliced lengthwise**

**4 ripe plum tomatoes, diced**

**1 envelope sazón Goya (page 6)**

**½ teaspoon kosher salt**

**8 ounces lightly salted fresh mozzarella
    cheese, grated**

**2 tablespoons whole milk**

**Freshly ground black pepper to taste**

The kind of food you never tire of, this savory, homey combination of potatoes, tomatoes, cheese, and scallions is my family's favorite side dish. The cooked potatoes can be left whole, quartered, or sliced, just as you like. It's great with simple grills and roasts, especially Colombian Pot Roast (page 140) or Onion-Chile Marinated Sirloin with *Chimichurri* (page 12).

**Place the potatoes** in a large pot and cover with cold salted water. Cover, bring to a boil, and cook until the potatoes are very soft but not falling apart, about 20 minutes. Drain the potatoes, transfer to a serving bowl, and set aside.

Heat the oil in a medium-size nonreactive heavy skillet over medium heat. Add the garlic, scallions, tomatoes, sazón, and salt and cook, stirring, until softened and translucent, 5 to 8 minutes. Gradually stir in the cheese and add the milk. Stir until incorporated and slightly thickened. Taste for salt and pepper. Pour the hot sauce over the potatoes and serve immediately.

# Peruvian Potatoes with Spicy Cheese Sauce (Papas a la Huancaina)

Makes 6 servings

2 pounds new potatoes, scrubbed

2 tablespoons olive oil

1 teaspoon finely minced garlic

2 scallions, white and pale green parts, thinly sliced

1 teaspoon turmeric

1/4 teaspoon cayenne pepper or yellow (*amarillo*) chile powder

8 ounces *queso blanco*, farmer cheese, or mild feta cheese, crumbled

6 tablespoons heavy cream

2 teaspoons Dijon mustard

Kosher salt and freshly ground black pepper to taste

12 brine-cured black olives, pitted

1/2 large red bell pepper, seeded and sliced into thin rings

*Papas a la Huancaina* is one of the most universal and popular dishes of Peruvian cuisine, although it became popular as recently as the nineteenth century. A *Huancaina* is a woman native to the province of Huancayo; one such woman fed this nourishing dish to some of the thousands of hungry workers who built Peru's mountain-spanning Central Railway through the Andes. According to legend, they returned the favor by naming the dish for her and bringing it back to their homes when the railway was finished, thus spreading it throughout the land. Recipes abound, but whether the savory sauce is thickened with egg yolks or cheese, yellowed with mustard or turmeric, or spiced with cayenne or Peruvian mirasol peppers, the result is invariably delicious.

When the dish is served cold, it becomes a sort of sublime potato salad; it's also a very satisfying summertime vegetarian entree. Sliced hard-boiled eggs and chopped parsley on top are very successful additions if desired. If serving cold, refrigerate the potatoes and sauce separately. Just before serving, whisk the sauce thoroughly, pour over the potatoes, and add the garnishes.

**In a large pot,** cover the potatoes with cold salted water and bring to a boil. Boil until cooked through but still firm, 10 to 15 minutes. Drain. When the potatoes are cool enough to handle, slice 1/4 inch thick or cut into quarters and arrange on a platter.

In a medium-size skillet, heat the olive oil over medium heat. Add the garlic, scallions, turmeric, and cayenne and cook, stirring, until softened, about 5 minutes. Add the cheese, cream, and mustard and cook, stirring constantly, until the cheese melts and the sauce is thick and yellow. Season with salt and pepper. Pour the hot sauce over the potatoes. Sprinkle the olives over the dish, then lay the rings of red pepper on top and serve.

# Yuca Fries

Makes 6 servings

**2 pounds frozen yuca (page 8)**

**6 cups Chicken Stock (page 32), canned
    low-sodium chicken broth, or salted
    water**

**Vegetable oil for frying**

**Kosher salt to taste**

**½ cup Braised Garlic-Thyme *Mojo* with
    Lime (page 20)**

Fresh yuca makes beautiful golden fries with a delicate flavor, much enhanced by a preliminary poaching in stock. These are particularly thirsty for a drizzle of Braised Garlic-Thyme *Mojo*.

**Place the yuca** in a large pot, add the stock, cover, and bring to a boil. Boil until softened but still firm, 20 to 30 minutes. Drain and let dry, or pat dry with paper towels. With your fingers, remove the tough, stringy cores from the yuca.

Preheat the oven to 250 degrees and put an oven-proof serving platter in the oven to heat. Heat the oil in a deep fryer according to the manufacturer's instructions (or heat 2 inches of oil in a deep, heavy pot) to about 365 degrees, hot enough to quickly cook a test piece of yuca. Working in batches to avoid crowding the pot, fry the yuca until golden. As it is cooked, drain on paper towels, sprinkle lightly with salt, and keep hot in the oven. Serve immediately, drizzled with *mojo*.

# Yuca Hash Browns

yuca hash browns

Makes 4 to 6 servings

3 tablespoons olive oil

1 pound cooked yuca (page 8),
   stringy cores discarded and cut into
   ½-inch dice

8 ounces shiitake or cremini
   mushrooms, sliced ¼ inch thick

½ cup fresh or frozen corn kernels (do
   not thaw)

½ cup thinly sliced scallions, white and
   pale green parts

½ cup seeded and diced ripe plum
   tomatoes

1 teaspoon roasted garlic (page 6)

½ teaspoon ground cumin

1 tablespoon chopped cilantro leaves

Kosher salt and freshly ground black
   pepper to taste

Yuca, also known as *cassava* and *manioc* in different languages and different centuries, is a starchy staple in Africa as well as in South America. This dish is a great way to get to know the versatile root vegetable. Some chefs mash their yuca, but I like it best poached and diced, then combined with strong flavorings and light textures. Yuca and garlic are an essential combination in the Latin kitchen.

**Heat the olive oil** in a large nonreactive skillet over medium-high heat. Add the remaining ingredients in order, stirring after each addition. Cook, stirring occasionally, until golden brown, 8 to 10 minutes. Serve immediately.

# Crisp Plantain Coins (*Patacones*)

*Makes 4 servings*

**Peanut oil for frying**
**2 large green plantains, peeled**
  **(page 5) and sliced ¼ inch thick on**
  **the diagonal or lengthwise**
**Kosher salt to taste**

*T*he word *patacón* doesn't refer only to these crisp, golden slices of fried plantain—it was also Spanish slang for the gold nuggets the *conquistadores* discovered in plenty on their arrival in the *Nuevo Mundo* of Latin America. It's an appropriate name, though—not only is their color golden but *patacones* are a highly prized staple of the Latin diet, under many different names. In Colombia, *patacones* are served with almost everything you can think of.

When I prepare *patacones* at my restaurant, I slice the plantains lengthwise—this adds to the dramatic presentation of my Ecuadoran Mixed Seafood Ceviche (page 65).

**Preheat the oven** to 250 degrees and put an ovenproof serving platter in the oven to heat.

Heat the oil in a deep fryer according to the manufacturer's instructions (or heat 2 inches of oil in a deep, heavy pot) to about 365 degrees, hot enough to quickly cook a test piece of plantain. Working in batches to avoid crowding the pot, fry the plantain slices until golden. As they are cooked, drain them on paper towels, sprinkle with salt, and keep hot in the oven. Serve immediately.

# Mashed Sweet Plantains (*Fufu*)

Makes 4 servings

2 very ripe plantains, peeled (page 5)
   and sliced ½ inch thick

1 cup Chicken Stock (page 32),
   Vegetable Stock (page 34), canned
   low-sodium broth, or salted water

2 tablespoons pure maple syrup or
   honey

1 tablespoon unsalted butter

3 tablespoons dry bread crumbs
   (optional)

Kosher salt to taste

*T*he sweet and starchy flavors and textures of *fufu*—mashed ripe plantains—make it real South American comfort food, not unlike our mashed potatoes. It is wonderful all by itself, under a savory stew, or with Colombian Red Beans (page 172) and fresh cilantro, or even for breakfast with a fried egg on top. Warm *fufu* even harmonizes with vanilla ice cream for a richly appealing dessert. The bread crumbs add a nice, subtle crunch to the mixture. You can tell when plantains are ready to be made into *fufu*—their skins will be completely black.

**Combine the plantains,** stock, and syrup in a medium-size saucepan, bring to a gentle boil, and cook until the plantains are soft, 15 to 25 minutes. Add water a little at a time, as needed, to keep the mixture from drying out. Scrape the mixture into a large bowl and mash with a potato masher to make a smooth, creamy puree. Add the butter and bread crumbs, if using, and mix well to combine. Season with salt. Serve immediately or scrape into a baking dish, cover with a sheet of aluminum foil, and keep hot in a 225-degree oven up to 1 hour.

# Sweet Plantain Rice

Makes 4 to 6 servings

2 very ripe plantains, peeled (page 5) and cut into ½-inch dice

2 tablespoons unsalted butter, melted

2 teaspoons olive oil

1 garlic clove, finely minced

1 cup long-grain rice, rinsed

2 cups Vegetable Stock (page 34) or water

½ teaspoon kosher salt

1 teaspoon firmly packed *panela* (page 5) or dark brown sugar

Freshly ground black pepper to taste

I've often thought that North American cooking, with its focus on breads and potatoes, is missing out on the pleasures of other starches. Plantains and rice are key elements in Latin cooking and nutrition—and they both happen to be delicious. Here I've combined them in a nutty, lightly sweet side dish that sets off both elements to perfection.

**Preheat the oven** to 375 degrees. In a medium-size baking dish, toss the plantains with the butter and bake, stirring once, until golden brown, 15 to 20 minutes.

Meanwhile, in a medium-size heavy saucepan, heat the oil over medium heat. Add the garlic and cook, stirring, until softened, about 3 minutes. Add the rice and stir to coat. Add the vegetable stock and salt and bring to a boil, then reduce the heat to as low as possible and cover tightly. Cook for 18 minutes without disturbing.

Meanwhile, in a large bowl, mash the roasted plantains with a potato masher. Add the cooked rice and *panela* and mix to combine. Keep hot in the oven, tightly covered, until ready to serve. Just before serving, fluff with a fork and season with salt and pepper.

# Roasted Corn and Garlic Rice

Makes 4 to 6 servings

2 teaspoons olive oil

1 cup long-grain rice, rinsed

2 cups Chicken Stock (page 32),
   Vegetable Stock (page 34), canned
   low-sodium broth, or water

1 teaspoon roasted garlic (page 6)

1 bay leaf

½ teaspoon kosher salt

1 cup roasted corn (page 5)

Freshly ground black pepper to taste

I don't know what I'd do without this side dish in my repertoire—it seems to go with everything. The rich flavor adds depth to light entrees like Salmon with Saffron (page 119) and Venezuelan Eggplant with Green Beans (page 116); the roasted notes complement grilled dishes like Garlic Shrimp and Pineapple Skewers (page 145) or Onion-Chile Marinated Sirloin with *Chimichurri* (page 152).

In a medium-size, heavy saucepan, heat the oil over medium heat. Add the rice and stir to coat. Add the stock, garlic, bay leaf, and salt and bring to a boil, then reduce the heat to as low as possible and cover tightly. Cook, undisturbed, for 13 minutes. Uncover, quickly stir in the roasted corn, replace the lid, and cook 7 minutes more. Keep covered until ready to serve. Just before serving, fluff with a fork and season with salt and pepper.

# Cartagena Coconut-Pineapple Rice (Arroz con Coco)

Makes 6 to 8 servings

1½ cups long-grain rice, rinsed

3½ cups unsweetened coconut milk (page 4)

¼ cup ¼-inch peeled fresh pineapple dice

1 teaspoon minced fresh mint leaves

1 teaspoon unsalted butter

½ teaspoon kosher salt

In Colombia, the dish that really says there's a Caribbean cook in the kitchen is *arroz con coco,* a fluffy, slightly sweet side dish that is much more popular than plain white rice in the region's capital of Cartagena. There are several versions of the dish, many of which include raisins; I find this too much like rice pudding for comfort. Some cooks toast the coconut before cooking, and some create the same caramelized effect with a dash of Coca-Cola in the cooking water! I prefer a harmonious accent of fresh pineapple, which is much less sweet than the canned kind.

**In a medium-size,** heavy saucepan with a tight-fitting lid, combine the rice and coconut milk. Cover, bring to a boil, stir once, and reduce the heat to as low as possible. Cook undisturbed until cooked through and dry, 20 to 25 minutes. Turn off the heat and scatter the pineapple and mint over the rice. Cover the pot and let stand for 5 to 15 minutes. Before serving, add the butter, fluff with a fork, and season with the salt.

# Black Beans and White Rice (*Moros*)

*Makes 8 servings*

3 tablespoons olive oil

2 garlic cloves, minced

2 cups long-grain white rice, rinsed

4 cups boiling water

2 teaspoons kosher salt

¼ cup fresh or frozen corn kernels (do not thaw)

¼ cup thinly sliced scallions, white and pale green parts

2 ripe plum tomatoes, seeded and diced

2 cups drained freshly cooked (page 3) or canned black beans

1 tablespoon unsalted butter

Freshly ground black pepper to taste

It's the black of the beans and the white of the rice that give this Cuban dish its full name of *Moros y Cristianos*, Muslims and Christians. The two religions were frequently at war during the turbulent period of the Spanish conquest of Latin America, so the name is hardly surprising—but black and white have a very happy, peaceful relationship in this dish. In fact, I even felt safe adding some other colors to the mix: red tomatoes, green scallions, and yellow corn kernels.

**In a medium-size,** heavy saucepan with a tight-fitting lid, heat the oil over medium-high heat. Add the garlic and cook, stirring, until softened, about 3 minutes. Add the rice and stir until evenly coated with oil. Add the boiling water and salt, cover, and bring to a boil. Reduce the heat to as low as possible and cook, undisturbed, for 18 minutes. Turn off the heat and scatter the corn, scallions, tomatoes, and beans on top of the rice. Cover the pot and let stand for 5 to 15 minutes. Before serving, add the butter, fluff with a fork, taste for salt and season with pepper.

# Colombian Red Beans (*Frijoles Rojos*)

*Makes 8 to 10 servings*

**2 pounds dried cranberry or pink beans, rinsed and picked over**

**2 pounds smoked ham hocks**

**2 large green plantains, peeled (page 5)**

**½ cup *Hogo* (page 11)**

**Kosher salt to taste**

My wife's grandmother, Marina, makes the most wonderful, deep-flavored bowls of beans I've ever had. As you see, this is a very simple recipe—the mark of a true family staple. She is a real stickler for tradition, even observing the old ritual of cutting up the plantains with her thumbnail instead of using a knife. All the *abuelas,* or grandmothers, swear that it makes a difference, but I don't agree. She looked so shocked when I suggested adding fresh cilantro to this recipe that I couldn't go through with it, but you should do what your own instincts (or your own grandmothers) dictate. Serve with white rice and *Patacones* (page 166) for a traditional Colombian lunch.

**Place the beans** in a large pot, cover with cold water, bring to a simmer, and cook, covered, until the beans are somewhat softened but still quite firm, about 1½ hours. Check the beans frequently to make sure they are covered with water; add more boiling water as needed.

Add the ham hocks to the pot. Cut or grate the plantains into very small chunks—less than ¼ inch—and add to the pot, then stir in ¼ cup of the *hogo.* Simmer, covered, adding more boiling water as needed, until the plantains and beans are cooked through, about 45 minutes more. Stir occasionally. Toward the end of the cooking, uncover the pot so that the mixture can thicken, and season with salt. Serve in bowls, topped with a spoonful of *hogo.*

# Gratin of Hearts of Palm (*Palmitos Gratinados*)

*Makes 4 to 6 servings*

**1 cup heavy cream**

**4 large eggs**

**1 tablespoon roasted garlic (page 6)**

**One 16-ounce can hearts of palm, drained, trimmed of any hard rinds, and cut into ½-inch dice**

**8 ounces Westphalian or other smoked ham, in one piece, cut into ¼-inch dice**

**2 ripe plum tomatoes, seeded and diced**

**1 teaspoon finely chopped cilantro leaves**

Hearts of palm, or *palmitos,* make a delicate alternative to potatoes in this flanlike side dish. Crunchy *palmitos* and rich orange palm oil (called *dendê*) are very common in Brazil, reflecting the strong African influence on that country's cooking. The only thing to be careful of in this simple, elegant dish is not to overcook the custard; remove it from the oven when the centers still "shimmy" a bit as you move the pan. They will continue to cook as they cool.

**Preheat the oven** to 350 degrees. In a small, heavy saucepan, whisk the cream, eggs, and garlic together. Bring to a simmer over medium-low heat and simmer gently for 5 minutes.

Meanwhile, divide the palm hearts among 4 to 6 ramekins. Sprinkle the ham evenly over the tops, then add the tomatoes, then the cilantro. Gently pour the cooked cream mixture into the ramekins. Arrange the ramekins in a roasting pan, then pour hot tap water around them until it comes halfway up the sides of the ramekins. Bake until the consistency is custardlike, about 30 minutes. Let cool briefly on a wire rack, then unmold onto serving plates.

# Desserts
# (Postres)

Flourless Chocolate Cake with Coffee Glaze

Frozen Chocolate Pudding with
Cashew Nuts

Espresso-Almond Brownies

Caramelized *Arequipe* Cheesecake

Amanda's Pineapple-Citrus Pound Cake
(*Mantecada de Amanda*)

Fresh Figs in Cinnamon Syrup with Fresh
Cheese (*Brevas con Queso*)

Berry Compote (*Dulce de Moras*)

Passionfruit Flan

Guava Pancakes

Sweet Raisin Tamales (*Envueltos de Mazorca*)

Vanilla–Brown Sugar Ice Cream (*Helado de
Vanilla con Panela*)

Fried *Churros* with Berry or Chocolate Sauce

Caramelized Ice Cream with Toasted
Almonds (*Helado de Cajeta*)

Blackberry Sorbet

Orange-Guava Butter Cookies

Caramelized Sugar Cookies (*Galletas de
Alfajores*)

# Flourless Chocolate Cake with Coffee Glaze

Makes one 9-inch cake

For the cake:

**8 ounces semisweet chocolate**

**½ cup (1 stick) unsalted butter, softened**

**3 large eggs, separated, at room temperature**

For the glaze:

**⅓ cup coffee liqueur, such as Kahlúa, or another flavored liqueur**

**⅓ cup water**

**⅓ cup sugar**

In seventeenth-century Europe, two exciting new drinks from Latin America—coffee and hot chocolate—suddenly became tremendously fashionable, spawning salons, coffee houses, and, of course, cafés all across the continent. Both were considered to have a wonderfully stimulating effect on the brain—and the libido. Chocolate (in the form of cacao beans) is indigenous to Latin America and has been drunk there, often as part of sacred ritual, since time immemorial. When Cortez arrived in Mexico and asked to see the treasures of the Aztecs, he wasn't led to a storehouse of gold; they took him instead to the royal cocoa plantation.

Today, both coffee and chocolate are popular drinks in Latin America; I've combined them in a simple, rich, irresistible dessert that resembles a fallen soufflé. You could, however, use another flavored liqueur for the glaze such as orange.

**Preheat the oven** to 425 degrees.

In the top of a double boiler over simmering (not boiling) water, melt the chocolate and butter together, stirring. Place the egg yolks in a large bowl. Very gradually add the chocolate mixture to the egg yolks, whisking constantly. Let cool slightly.

In another large bowl, whip the egg whites until stiff (but not dry) peaks form and fold gently into the chocolate-egg mixture.

Butter and lightly flour a 9-inch springform pan. Scrape the batter into the pan, smooth the top, and bake until set, about 15 minutes. Cool on a wire rack for 15 minutes and remove the sides of the pan.

While the cake is cooling, make the glaze: Combine the liqueur, water, and sugar in a small saucepan and simmer, brushing the sugar crystals as they form down from the sides of the pan with a pastry brush dipped in cold water. When the glaze is syrupy, brush it over the surface of the warm cake. Let the cake cool to room temperature before serving.

## Frozen Chocolate Pudding with Cashew Nuts

*Makes 4 to 6 servings*

**1 cup cashew nuts**

**2 ounces semisweet chocolate**

**¼ cup coffee liqueur, such as Kahlúa**

**5 large eggs, separated**

**1 cup chilled heavy cream**

Cashew nuts, or *caju,* make regular appearances in the African-influenced cuisine of Brazil. I love their rich, toasty crunch, especially as a foil to a dark, creamy chocolate mousse.

**Preheat the oven** to 350 degrees. Spread the cashew nuts on a baking sheet and bake just until golden and toasted, 3 to 7 minutes. Let cool, then coarsely chop in a food processor or with a large knife.

In the top of a double boiler over simmering (not boiling) water, stir the chocolate until melted. Whisk in the coffee liqueur and turn off the heat, but leave the double boiler on the stove.

In a large bowl, whisk the egg yolks until foamy and light yellow, then gently whisk them into the chocolate mixture. In an electric mixer, whip the egg whites until stiff (but not dry) peaks form. Clean and dry the beaters. In a medium-size bowl, whip the cream with the mixer until stiff (but not dry) peaks form. With a rubber spatula, gently fold the whipped cream into the chocolate mixture, then fold in the egg whites. Fold in the cashews.

Divide the mixture among 4 to 6 soufflé cups, ramekins, or coffee mugs. Cover with plastic wrap and refrigerate 3 to 4 hours or overnight. Serve cold.

# Espresso-Almond Brownies

*Makes one 10-inch pan of brownies*

1⅔ cups sugar

½ cup (1 stick) unsalted butter, softened

1 tablespoon water

2 large eggs

1 tablespoon pure vanilla extract

1⅓ cups all-purpose flour

¾ cup unsweetened cocoa powder, preferably Dutch-process

2 tablespoons finely ground espresso coffee

1½ teaspoons baking powder

½ teaspoon kosher salt

1 cup semisweet chocolate chips

⅓ cup slivered almonds, toasted (optional; page 8)

As long ago as A.D. 400, the Maya of Mexico were drinking a ceremonial brew of chocolate mixed with chile or honey as a tribute to the gods who had provided them with the wonderfully sustaining cocoa tree (*cacahuaquchtl* in Mayan). It wasn't until Spanish nuns arrived in the sixteenth century, intent on making converts of the population, that the seductive mixture of cocoa, vanilla, and sugar that we know as chocolate was achieved.

Even today, chocolate isn't nearly as popular as a dessert in Latin America as it is elsewhere in the world. Latinos seem to prefer milk- and fruit-based sweets. However, the appetite of my New York City customers (and of my daughter, Amanda) for chocolate seems inexhaustible. These brownies are great with either of the ice creams in this chapter.

**Preheat the oven** to 350 degrees.

In a large bowl, beat the sugar, butter, and water together until fluffy. Add the eggs and vanilla and mix just until combined. In a medium-size bowl, combine the flour, cocoa, espresso, baking powder, and salt. Gradually add the dry ingredients to the wet, mixing well until smooth. Mix in the chocolate chips and almonds, if using.

Butter a 10-inch square baking pan or line with parchment paper. Pour the batter in, smooth the top, and bake until the center is just set and a tester comes out clean, about 35 minutes. Let cool 10 minutes before serving.

## Caramelized Arequipe Cheesecake

*Makes one 9-inch cake*

**Two 8-ounce cans sweetened condensed milk (do not open)**

**One 8-ounce package cream cheese, at room temperature**

**6 large eggs**

**2 cups heavy cream**

Like many Latinos, I learned this method of caramelizing condensed milk when I was a child. In Colombia, we made flan with it, but it's beautifully suited to New York–style cheesecake. Caramelized milk, especially goat's milk, is a popular sweet all over South America (called *dulce de leche, cajeta, arequipe, manjarblanco,* and any number of other names; children eat it by the spoonful), but this makes an excellent substitute. Serve the cake cool, not cold, for the best flavor.

**Caramelize the milk** according to the instructions on page 7.

Preheat the oven to 325 degrees. In a food processor or electric mixer, process the cream cheese until soft. With the motor running, add the eggs, cream, and caramelized condensed milk. Scrape the mixture into a 9-inch pie dish and place the dish in a roasting pan. Add hot tap water around the dish until it comes halfway up the sides. Bake, uncovered, 60 to 70 minutes. To test for doneness, insert a knife or skewer in the center of the cake—it should come out clean. The top should be dry and golden. Let the cake rest 1 hour to firm up, then serve or refrigerate. If refrigerated, let the cake sit at room temperature for at least half an hour before serving.

# Amanda's Pineapple-Citrus Pound Cake (Mantecada de Amanda)

*Makes one 9-inch cake*

For the cake:

2 cups freshly squeezed orange Juice

1 cup sugar

¾ cup (1½ sticks) unsalted butter, softened

6 large eggs, separated, at room temperature

2 tablespoons orange liqueur, such as Grand Marnier

1 cup all-purpose flour

1 teaspoon baking powder

For the topping:

1 pound fresh pineapple, peeled and cut into 1-inch dice (about 2½ cups)

3 tablespoons sugar

¼ cup water

My little daughter, Amanda, loves the simple, light pound cake we find at all the bakeries on our visits to Colombia. This differs a bit from a North American pound cake—the egg whites are whipped stiff and folded into the batter, creating a lighter, fluffier texture for the finished cake.

**In a small, nonreactive saucepan,** simmer the orange juice until it is reduced to ½ cup. Set aside to cool.

Preheat the oven to 350 degrees. In a large glass or ceramic bowl, beat the sugar into the butter until fluffy. Add the egg yolks, reduced orange juice, and orange liqueur and mix well. Gradually mix in the flour and baking powder. In another large bowl, whip the egg whites until stiff (but not dry) peaks form. Fold gently into the batter.

Lightly butter a 9-inch square or round baking pan, scrape the batter into it, and smooth the top. Bake until a cake tester or skewer inserted in the center comes out clean, 30 to 40 minutes.

Meanwhile, make the topping: Combine the pineapple, sugar, and water in a nonreactive medium-size saucepan and bring to a simmer. Simmer, stirring occasionally, until the pineapple is caramelized and light brown, 8 to 10 minutes. Brush the sugar crystals as they form down from the sides of the pan occasionally with a pastry brush dipped in cold water. Set aside the pineapple to cool to room temperature.

When the cake comes out of the oven, let cool on a wire rack for 15 minutes. If desired, turn out onto a serving plate. Spread the topping over the cake and let cool to room temperature before serving.

## Fresh Figs in Cinnamon Syrup with Fresh Cheese (*Brevas con Queso*)

Makes 4 servings

**2 cups water**

**1 cup firmly packed *panela* (page 5) or dark brown sugar**

**One 4-inch cinnamon stick**

**4 cloves**

**12 small fresh figs**

**12 ounces very fresh *queso blanco*, unsalted mozzarella, mascarpone, or farmer cheese**

*B*revas are much more popular in Latin America than plain old figs are in North America. In Colombia, figs are in season all year-round—but in Jackson Heights, a large Colombian (and Indian, Peruvian, and Dominican) community in Queens, the local restaurants content themselves with jars of preserved figs from the homeland. I prefer to wait until the fresh figs are available in the summer months.

Sweet figs and fresh cheese is a very common dessert combination in Bogotá. The white-coated women who staff the city's pristine cheesemakers' shops keep a supply of candied *brevas* on hand for stuffing with the day's new cheese. You can replicate the effect by taking simultaneous bites of cheese and figs, both drizzled with fragrant syrup.

**In a medium-size nonreactive saucepan,** combine the water, *panela* or brown sugar, cinnamon, and cloves and bring to a simmer over medium heat. Cook, stirring occasionally, 10 to 15 minutes, until the mixture has the consistency of a thin syrup. Add the figs and simmer 15 minutes more. Turn off the heat and let cool at least 15 minutes before serving. Slice or spoon the cheese onto serving plates. Place three figs on each plate and drizzle the syrup over the cheese and the figs.

# Berry Compote (*Dulce de Moras*)

Makes 4 servings

**2 cups fresh ripe *moras* (page 191),
   raspberries, or blackberries**

**Zest of ½ orange, cut into strips**

**2 tablespoons sugar**

**½ cup water**

*I*n the sweet, heady days of berry season, make quantities of this simple compote and freeze for chillier days. *Dulce de moras* is good warm, cold, or at room temperature, on top of ice cream, fresh cheese, or cheesecake—or in a bowl all by itself with Caramelized Sugar Cookies (page 193) for dipping.

**In a medium-size nonreactive saucepan,** combine all the ingredients and bring to a simmer over medium heat. Let simmer for 5 minutes. Let cool to room temperature and serve (or refrigerate, covered, for up to four days, or freeze for up to six months).

# Passionfruit Flan

Adding frozen passionfruit puree to flan makes a lighter and fresher version of the creamy Latin classic. You may notice that this differs from a classic flan recipe—the mixture isn't cooked before baking. I prefer the smoother, lighter texture of this method. Passionfruit pulp is easily found at any Latin market and many gourmet shops. Mango pulp would make an excellent substitute if necessary. Don't skip the straining—it removes fibers that can ruin the texture of the flan.

*Makes 4 servings*

*For the caramel:*

**1 cup water**

**¼ cup sugar**

*For the flan:*

**6 large eggs, at room temperature**

**½ cup heavy cream**

**½ cup whole milk**

**3 tablespoons sugar**

**1 cup fresh or thawed frozen passionfruit or mango pulp, processed until smooth in a blender or food processor**

**Make the caramel:** Combine the water and sugar in a small, heavy saucepan over medium heat. As soon as the mixture begins to bubble, stir it with a wooden spoon and reduce the heat to low. Cook, stirring frequently to prevent burning and washing the sugar crystals as they form down from the sides of the pan with a pastry brush dipped in cold water, until medium brown, about 15 minutes. Divide the caramel among the four soufflé cups and set them aside to cool.

Preheat the oven to 325 degrees. In a large bowl, combine the eggs, cream, and milk with a whisk. Stir in the sugar and passionfruit. Strain the mixture through a fine-mesh sieve. Pour the mixture into the soufflé cups and arrange them in a roasting pan. Add hot tap water around the soufflé cups until it comes halfway up their sides. Bake for 45 minutes, carefully rotating the pan after 20 minutes to ensure even cooking. When the centers are soft but firm, the flan is done. Let the cups cool in the pan, remove them from the water, cover with plastic wrap (pressing the wrap against the surface of the flan to prevent a skin from forming), and refrigerate 4 to 24 hours.

When ready to serve, run a knife around the edge of each soufflé cup and flip onto a plate. If the flans stick to the cups, place them in a pan of hot water for 10 minutes to loosen the caramel.

Guava paste is one of the Colombian kitchen's most versatile ingredients. Rolled into cookies, layered with flaky pastry, or transformed into candy kisses with moist shredded coconut, guava paste has a lovely smooth texture. In France, buttery crepes are often flavored with orange liqueur; guava has a similar balance of sweet and sour. The first crepe is usually destined for the garbage can, but you'll quickly get the knack.

## Guava Pancakes

Makes 4 servings

4 large eggs, at room temperature, separated

12 ounces guava paste, at room temperature

1 cup warm water

½ cup all-purpose flour

1 teaspoon unsalted butter

**In a large bowl,** whip the egg whites until stiff (but not dry) peaks form. In a small bowl, whisk the egg yolks together. In another large bowl, whisk the guava paste and water together until smooth. While whisking gently, gradually sift the flour into the guava mixture through a sifter or a sieve, stirring to combine. Add the egg yolks and mix to combine. Gently fold the egg whites into the batter.

Heat a nonstick 7-inch skillet over medium-high heat. Pour in about 3 tablespoons of the batter, then quickly tilt the skillet so the batter evenly coats the bottom of the pan. Cook until the bottom browns, 30 to 45 seconds. Turn the crepe gently with a spatula or tongs, then cook another 15 seconds. If the crepe seems to be sticking, add the butter to the skillet and melt before proceeding. As you cook the crepes, serve immediately or stack them between layers of waxed paper to prevent sticking. Serve warm.

# Sweet Raisin Tamales (*Envueltos de Mazorca*)

*Makes 8 to 10 envueltos*

**2 cups fine-ground white or yellow cornmeal**

**2 cups boiling water**

**1 teaspoon kosher salt**

**¼ cup white or firmly packed dark brown sugar**

**2 tablespoons fresh goat cheese**

**½ cup dark raisins or dried cherries, plumped in boiling water, drained, and chopped**

**8 to 10 fresh or frozen banana leaves or sheets of parchment paper, 12 × 15 inches each**

**8 to 10 thin strips banana leaf or kitchen string for tying**

You can taste the Latin love of corn in this simple dessert—essentially a dessert *tamal* with dried fruit.

**Place the cornmeal** in a large bowl and add the water. Mix until the mixture holds together and is soft and faintly sticky to the touch; add more boiling water or cornmeal if necessary. Mix in the salt, sugar, cheese, and raisins. Let rest, covered, for 15 minutes.

Wipe a banana leaf clean with a clean, damp kitchen cloth and lay it lengthwise on your work surface, with the grain running from left to right. Mound about ¼ cup of the filling in the center of the leaf. As if wrapping a present, fold the top down over the filling, pressing lightly, then fold the bottom up to cover. Fold the ends into the center and turn the *envuelto* over. Again as if wrapping a present, tie securely closed. Repeat with remaining filling and wrappers.

Arrange a steamer in a pot with a tight-fitting lid filled with a couple of inches of water. Bring to a boil (the water should not touch the steamer), place the *envueltos* in the steamer, and steam until heated through and firm, 30 to 45 minutes. Serve still wrapped and let your guests carefully cut the *envueltos* open.

# Vanilla-Brown Sugar Ice Cream (Helado de Vanilla con Panela)

Makes about 3 quarts

3 cups whole milk

3 cups heavy cream

2 vanilla beans, split lengthwise

1 cup granulated sugar

½ cup firmly packed *panela* (page 5) or dark brown sugar

16 large egg yolks, at room temperature

The history of Latin America often intersects with the history of the world's love for sugar. Sugarcane was introduced to Brazil by Spanish conquerors/entrepreneurs in the sixteenth century and quickly spread across the continent. Thousands upon thousands of slaves were brought from Africa by plantation owners in need of free labor in the sugarcane fields—thus changing the face and food of the continent forever. In Peru, it was workers from China who toiled in the cane fields.

Colombia's national drink, *aguardiente,* is distilled from sugarcane sap; *panela,* Colombia's most common form of cooking sugar, is crystallized sugarcane sap. Hard and brown, *panela* comes in loaves and in bricks. We usually dissolve it in water before using, but that's not necessary here.

**In a large saucepan,** combine the milk and cream. Scrape out the "caviar" (the seeds) from the vanilla beans and add it to the milk mixture. Add the sugars and heat the mixture to a simmer over medium-low heat. Simmer, stirring occasionally, until the mixture has thickened somewhat, 20 to 25 minutes.

Put the egg yolks in a large bowl and whisk lightly. Very gradually whisk the hot milk mixture into the yolks, going very slowly at the beginning to avoid scrambling the eggs. Freeze the mixture in an ice cream maker according to the manufacturer's instructions and serve.

# Fried *Churros* with Berry or Chocolate Sauce

*Makes 4 to 6 servings*

*For the berry sauce:*

**1 cup pureed blackberries or raspberries, strained**

**2 cups water**

**½ to ¾ cup granulated sugar, to taste**

*For the chocolate sauce:*

**3 ounces semisweet chocolate**

**1½ teaspoons granulated sugar**

**⅓ cup heavy cream**

**1½ tablespoons coffee liqueur, such as Kahlúa**

*C*hurros is the Mexican name for a dessert that is actually popular all over Latin America—and all over the world. Deep-fried dough with a sweet topping seems to be a universal taste, from Pennsylvania to Patagonia. In Lima, street vendors sell *picarones*—thin rounds of fried dough drizzled with honey flavored with cinnamon. And *churros* with hot chocolate is a popular breakfast. These sweet and airy puffs are delicious when eaten quickly after they come out of the fryer; the oil should be very hot so that the puffs are crisped without absorbing oil. Note that you'll need a pastry tube for squeezing the batter into the oil.

I like to stack the churros into a square "log cabin" on each plate, with two logs per side, for serving. Drizzle with either sauce or both!

**Make the berry sauce:** Combine all the ingredients in a small nonreactive saucepan and simmer over medium-low heat until thickened. Keep warm.

Make the chocolate sauce: Combine the chocolate, sugar, and cream in a small, heavy saucepan and

**To make the churros:**

3 tablespoons granulated sugar

2 cups water

3 tablespoons unsalted butter

2½ cups all-purpose flour

Pinch of kosher salt

2 large eggs, at room temperature

Vegetable oil for frying

**To serve:**

½ cup superfine sugar

Fresh mint leaves

melt over low heat, stirring constantly until smooth. Turn off the heat and stir in the coffee liqueur. Keep warm.

Make the *churros:* In a medium-size saucepan, combine the granulated sugar, water, and butter and bring to a boil over medium-high heat. Stirring with a sturdy whisk, add all the flour at once and stir quickly until smooth. Add the salt. Turn off the heat and let rest for 2 minutes, then beat in the eggs one at a time.

Heat the oil in a deep fryer according to the manufacturer's instructions or heat 3 inches of oil in a deep, heavy pot to 365 degrees.

Spread the superfine sugar out on a plate.

Ladle the batter into a pastry tube fitted with a ½-inch-wide ridged tip. Working in batches if necessary to avoid crowding, squeeze 3-inch lengths of batter into the hot oil and cook until golden. Quickly drain on paper towels and roll in the sugar while still warm. Serve immediately, drizzled with both sauces and garnished with mint leaves.

# Caramelized Ice Cream with Toasted Almonds (*Helado de Cajeta*)

*Makes about 2 quarts*

**One 8-ounce can sweetened condensed milk (do not open)**

**2 cups whole milk**

**2 cups heavy cream**

**½ cup sugar**

**10 large egg yolks**

**1 teaspoon pure vanilla extract**

**½ cup almonds, toasted (page 8) and finely ground in a food processor**

*Cajeta* is yet another name for the sweet caramelized milk that is the basis for many beloved Latin desserts. The caramel flavor here blends beautifully with the toastiness of the almonds and the creamy vanilla of the ice cream.

**Caramelize the milk** according to the instructions on page 7.

In a medium-size saucepan, combine the whole milk, cream, and sugar and heat to a simmer over medium-low heat. Let simmer, stirring occasionally, until the mixture has thickened somewhat, 20 to 25 minutes. Place the egg yolks and vanilla in a large bowl and whisk lightly. Very gradually whisk the hot milk mixture into the yolks, going very slowly at the beginning to avoid cooking the eggs. Mix in the caramelized condensed milk and ground almonds. Freeze the mixture in an ice cream maker according to the manufacturer's instructions and serve.

# Blackberry Sorbet

Though they are clearly of the same family, no North American blackberry has quite the same intensity of flavor as a Colombian *mora;* it's one of my favorites among the hundreds of exciting fruits available in the markets of Bogotá. Deep purple and as big as your thumb, *moras* are sold in this country in the form of a frozen puree, but fresh or frozen blackberries will also work in this recipe; other fruits, like mango, peach, and guava, can be substituted or mixed in as well.

Makes about 4 cups

2 cups sugar

3½ cups water

4 cups *moras* or blackberries, fresh or
    thawed frozen, or 3 cups thawed
    frozen *mora* pulp

Freshly squeezed juice of 1 lemon

**Combine the sugar and water** in a medium-size saucepan and cook over medium-low heat, stirring occasionally, until the sugar has dissolved. Set aside to cool to room temperature.

Meanwhile, process the berries in a food processor or blender until smooth. Pour through a fine-mesh strainer to remove the seeds. Transfer the sugar syrup to a large glass or ceramic bowl and add the strained puree and lemon juice. Stir to blend and refrigerate until well chilled, about 2 hours. Freeze in an ice cream maker according to the manufacturer's instructions or pour the mixture into a roasting pan and freeze for 4 to 5 hours. Check the mixture every hour and whisk it well to break up the ice crystals. When it is slushy, transfer to a serving bowl and refrigerate an additional 30 minutes before serving.

# Orange-Guava Butter Cookies

**A** Latin take on the classic "thumbprint" butter-and-jam cookies, this crumbly cookie is based on an old family recipe. I figured out an easier way to make them when my daughter, Amanda, got bored halfway through the laborious spreading, stuffing, and rolling process of the original, and I had to finish the whole batch by myself!

*Makes about 3 dozen cookies*

1 cup freshly squeezed orange juice

½ cup sugar

1 cup (2 sticks) unsalted butter, softened

1 teaspoon pure vanilla extract

2 large egg yolks

2¼ cups all-purpose flour

1 teaspoon baking powder

6 ounces guava paste (page 4), cut into ¼-inch dice

**In a nonreactive small saucepan,** simmer the orange juice over medium-low heat until reduced to 2 tablespoons. Set aside to cool.

In a large glass or ceramic bowl, beat the sugar and butter together until fluffy. Add the reduced orange juice, vanilla, and egg yolks and mix to combine. Gradually add the flour and baking powder, mixing until smooth. Cover with plastic wrap and refrigerate for 30 minutes.

Preheat the oven to 350 degrees. Shape the dough into 1-inch balls and place them 2 inches apart on ungreased cookie sheets. Use your thumb to make an imprint in the center of each cookie. Bake for 10 minutes, then remove from the oven and quickly place a piece of guava paste in each imprint. Return to the oven to finish baking until the cookies are golden brown, 2 to 4 minutes more. Let cool on wire racks.

# Caramelized Sugar Cookies (*Galletas de Alfajores*)

Makes about 3 dozen cookies

**One 8-ounce can sweetened condensed milk (do not open)**

**1 cup (2 sticks) unsalted butter, softened**

**3 tablespoons sugar**

**1 cup cornstarch**

**1½ cups all-purpose flour**

*T*he cornstarch in these cookies makes them especially crisp and melting. They're wonderful with hot *café con leche*.

**Caramelize the milk** according to the instructions on page 7.

Preheat the oven to 350 degrees. In a large bowl, beat the butter and sugar together until fluffy. Add the caramelized condensed milk and mix. In a small bowl, combine the cornstarch and flour. Gradually stir the dry ingredients into the wet, mixing until smooth. Lightly flour your work surface and roll out the dough ⅛ inch thick. Cut the dough into cookies with cookie cutters and place 1 inch apart on ungreased baking sheets. Bake until golden brown, 10 to 12 minutes, and let cool on wire racks.

# Sources

For Latin ingredients:
La Preferida, Inc.
3400 West 35th Street
Chicago, IL 60632
773-254-7200

Tropic-Good Distributors
33-60 55th Street
Woodside, NY 11377
718-533-7181

For canned chipotles:
International Hot Foods, Inc.
905 N. California Avenue
Chicago, IL 60622
800-505-9999

For fresh herbs:
The Herb Farm
32804 Issaquah-Fall City Road
Fall City, WA 98024
800-866-HERB

For spices:
Penzey's Spice House
1921 S. West Avenue
Waukesha, WI 53186
414-574-0277

For fresh queso blanco and
mozzarella cheeses:
The Mozzarella Company
2944 Elm Street
Dallas, TX 75226
800-798-2954

For all kinds of gourmet and
imported products, especially
dried beans:
Dean & DeLuca
800-221-7714
or
Balducci's
800-BALDUCCI'S
or
Williams-Sonoma
415-421-4242

For kitchen equipment:
The Chef's Catalog
3215 Commercial Avenue
Northbrook, IL 60062-1900
800-338-3232
or
Williams-Sonoma
415-421-4242

# Index

-orange butter cookies,
192
pancakes, 185
in plantain-raisin muffins, 43

## h

ham:
    in Cuban sandwich, 45
    in gratin of hearts of palm,
        173
hash browns:
    shrimp and lobster, 125
    yuca, 165
*helado:*
    *de cajeta,* 190
    *de vanilla con panela,* 187
herbs, Colombian rice with
    pork loin, potatoes
    and, 136–137
*hogo,* 11
    aromatic braised oxtail with
        yuca, potatoes and, 112
    black bean soup with, 94
honey-chipotle *arepas,* 38

## i

ice cream:
    caramelized, with toasted
        almonds, 190
    in grilled plantains stuffed
        with guava, 153
    vanilla–brown sugar, 187
ingredients, notes on, 3–8

## j

jalapeño pepper(s):
    chilled melon soup with
        fresh, 101

in chorizo, artichoke
    and three-bean salad,
    84
roast chicken with yuca
    and, 132

## l

lemon, in citrus-chipotle salsa,
    14
lentils, arugula salad with
    plantains and, in
    roasted red onion
    vinaigrette, 86
lime(s):
    braised garlic-thyme *mojo*
        with, 20
    in citrus mayonnaise, 31
    cocktails, Brazilian, 54
    in grilled steak marinated in
        citrus, 150
    in pisco sours, 53
lobster:
    and black bean risotto,
        Martha's, 124
    in New World paella,
        126–127
    and shrimp hash browns,
        125
*lomo saltado,* 142

## m

main dishes, 113–142
mango:
    barbecue sauce, 21
    -chayote salsa, 15
    mimosas, 56
    vinaigrette, 23
*mantecada de Amanda,* 181
marmalade, citrus, barbecued
    ribs with, 148

mayonnaise:
    chipotle, 30
    citrus, 31
melon soup with fresh
        jalapeño, chilled, 101
mimosas, mango, 56
*mojo,* braised garlic-thyme,
        with lime, 20
*moras:*
    in berry compote, 183
    in blackberry sorbet, 191
*Moros,* 171
muffins:
    guava, 44
    plantain-raisin, 43
mushroom(s), shiitake:
    ceviche with scallions,
        fresh, 67
    in pan-roasted red snapper
        with garbanzos and
        greens, 120
    in quick chicken stew with
        corn, 108
    in spicy vegetable
        empanadas, 76–77
    in summer vegetable tart,
        115
    in vegetable-stuffed *arepas,*
        49
    in Venezuelan eggplant
        with green beans,
        116
    in yuca hash browns,
        165
mushrooms, oyster, and
        wilted spinach,
        caramelized salmon
        fillets with, 118
mussels:
    in Honduran fish stew
        with yuca and
        coconut, 105
    in New World paella,
        126–127

## O

onion(s):
-chile marinated sirloin
with *chimichurri*, 152
Peruvian stir-fried beef
with, 142
-tomato relish, grilled steak
with, 151
-tomato sauce, 11
onion(s), red:
roasted, vinaigrette, 27
roasted, vinaigrette, arugula
salad with lentils and
plantains in, 86
orange(s):
in Amanda's pineapple-
citrus pound cake,
181
in barbecued ribs with
citrus marmalade,
148
in citrus-chipotle salsa, 14
in citrus mayonnaise, 31
in grilled steak marinated in
citrus, 150
-guava butter cookies,
192
in sparkling fruit punch,
58
vinaigrette, 24
oxtail, aromatic braised, with
yuca, potatoes and
*hogo,* 112

## P

paella, New World, 126–127
*paella Nuevo Mundo,* 126–127
palm, hearts of, gratin of,
173
*palmitos gratinados,* 173

*palomilla,* 150
pancakes, guava, 185
*pan de queso de Brasil,* 42
*papas:*
*chorreadas,* 162
*a la Huancaina,* 163
*saladas,* 161
papaya:
salsa, hot, 16
salsa, hot, marinated tuna
steaks with, 147
in sparkling fruit punch, 58
*parilla, a la,* 143–153
parsley:
fish baked in fresh tangerine
juice and, 121
-garlic crust, chicken
empanadas with,
74–75
passionfruit:
*batidas,* 55
flan, 184
*patacones,* 166
peanut sauce, spicy, chicken,
pork and potatoes in,
110
peas:
in Colombian rice with
pork loin, potatoes and
herbs, 136–137
in hearty barley-vegetable
soup with avocado, 97
in Martha's black bean and
lobster risotto, 124
in summer vegetable tart,
115
pepper:
sauce, fresh hot, 9
sauce with avocado, fresh
hot, 10
pepper, black, romaine-
pineapple salad with
yogurt and, 87
pepper, chipotle, *see* chipotle

pepper, jalapeño, *see* jalapeño
pepper(s)
pesto, cilantro, 19
grilled swordfish with, 146
*pinchos:*
*de camaron y piña,* 145
*de carne,* 149
pineapple:
-almond salsa, 13
-citrus pound cake,
Amanda's, 181
-coconut rice, Cartagena,
170
in cucumber and chayote
slaw, 85
and garlic shrimp skewers,
145
-romaine salad with yogurt
and black pepper, 87
in sparkling fruit punch,
58
in tuna ceviche with
coconut, 64
*pisco* sours, 53
plantain(s):
arugula salad with lentils
and, in roasted red
onion vinaigrette, 86
coins, crisp, 166
in Colombian red beans,
172
mashed sweet, 167
-raisin muffins, 43
—red bean soup with red
wine and cilantro,
93
in red snapper soup, 104
rice, sweet, 168
and shrimp tamales, 79
soup, Clota's, 95
in spicy vegetable
empanadas, 76–77
stuffed with guava, grilled,
153